Psalm 103:17-18

Praise for *Winning Begins at Home!*

Every leader needs a reminder and a strategy to win beyond work. Thankfully, Randy Gravitt gives us both in *Winning Begins at Home*. This book is a blueprint to building a great family!
—Dr. John C. Maxwell, #1 New York Times Bestselling Author, Founder of Maxwell Leadership

Randy Gravitt presents a simple strategy to help you win where it matters most. When you win at home, you are a winner. If you care about your family, read this book!
—Jon Gordon, 15x Bestselling Author of *The One Truth* and *The Energy Bus*

Winning Begins at Home is a must-read for leaders seeking unity and reconciliation in their home and work lives. Randy Gravitt takes readers on a guided journey, encouraging self-reflection in the practice of loving and living each day.
—Dr. Vanita Boswell, CEO, The VALO Group; Executive Producer, Netflix Original Documentary *Rooting for Roona*

Our families deserve our very best effort. In *Winning Begins at Home*, Randy Gravitt gives us a story to inspire and a strategy to follow. Whether you are just starting a family or need a reset, this book is a great place to start. Dig in!
—Len Vanden Bos, Team Chaplain, Buffalo Bills

I've known Randy for thirteen years, and we've leaned into each other for encouragement, strength, and hope. Randy has been consistently dependable with his messaging and his servant heart. Everyone loves a good story, and Randy can weave a story! If winning does not begin at home, losing will. *Winning Begins at Home* is a home run!
—Clint Hurdle, Former MLB World Series Manager and N. L. Manager of the Year

I have witnessed Randy's excellent leadership firsthand. One thing is clear, he prioritizes his faith and his family. In *Winning Begins at Home*, you'll glean insights into life and leadership from Randy's years of real-life experience. If you want to win outside of work, you should read this book!

—Shannon Miles, Board Chair and Cofounder, BELAY Solutions

The message of *Winning Begins at Home* needs to be heard and applied—urgently. In my work, from the US to Africa, I have seen firsthand that, when families don't thrive, it causes pain and trauma that lasts for generations. If we want to build a better future for our kids, it starts with strong families. Randy gives us a powerful roadmap for that journey!

—Justin Miller, Cofounder and CEO, Untold

Randy resonates with our team like no one else. His way and style create thoughtfulness and connect the learning to our everyday lives. The content is quite "sticky," helping you remember and utilize it in your everyday life. Randy has been coaching our team for over ten years, and we could not have made a better choice. He supports our strategy of developing a strong culture that promotes doing the right thing, the right way, every time. *Winning Begins at Home* continues that tradition in a most thoughtful and meaningful way. Every leader should read this book! Thank you, Randy.

—Tim Pollard, President and COO, Arrow Exterminators

Randy Gravitt unveils the secret to success in *Winning Begins at Home*. This unforgettable story conveys a message that will change your life, and it lands like a right-handed haymaker from Mike Tyson. A story with this clarity and power could only be told by someone who lives these principles each day. Thank you, Randy, for this gift.

—Billy Potter, CEO, Snellings Walters Insurance Agency

We are always looking for valuable resources that will help the coaches we serve. Randy's book hits a home run. I found it to be incredibly insightful and challenging in my own life as well. As I journeyed through the life of his character, John Williams, a Little League coach, it caused me to reflect on my own life as a leader who desires to be successful in my home as well as my work. *Winning Begins at Home* is an engaging and entertaining read. It inspired me to consider my choices and how I live relationally with my family and my team. I highly recommend it!

—Debbie Jobe, Chief Advancement Officer,
Fellowship of Christian Athletes

Randy Gravitt has "hit for the cycle" when it comes to his new book *Winning Begins at Home*. I have known Randy for ten years. He is a great leader, coach, husband, father, and role model. No one could be a better expert on what it looks like to win at home and in the professional world.

—Frank Windsor, President, Rinnai America

After years of close friendship with Randy, I have seen the wisdom in these pages lived out in his life and his family's. I'm thankful Randy has taken the time to capture these timeless principles in an approachable and easy-to-read parable that will encourage and guide future generations in navigating a busy world.

—David Millican, Officer Vice President,
Restaurant Development, Chick-fil-A Inc.

Winning Begins at Home speaks to the desire in every heart to connect with love and loved ones, and it speaks to what every child and spouse hungers for in that connection. Randy really does fulfill the old adage: "Give someone a fish, you feed them for a day. Teach someone to fish, and you feed them for a lifetime." The book gives story, steps, and outcome assurances. Randy offers the reader a very doable, lifetime manual that can leave a legacy of love in its wake. Well done! Thank you.

—Dr Chip Dodd, Author of *The Voice of the Heart*

Is there anything more important than winning at home? Is there anything more difficult to do? Everyone knows that no is the answer to both of those questions, yet few of us know how to make real progress. In *Winning Begins at Home*, Randy provides us a pathway to victory. The story is relatable, and the wisdom offered in it is eternal.

—Shane Duffey, Director of *NewSpring* Network

WINNING
BEGINS
AT HOME

WINNING *BEGINS* AT HOME

A STRATEGY TO WIN BEYOND WORK

BY RANDY GRAVITT

Winning Begins at Home: A Strategy to Win beyond Work—A Leadership Parable

Copyright © 2024 by Randy Gravitt

All rights reserved. No part of this publication may be reproduced, stored in a retrieval system, or transmitted in any form by any means, electronic, mechanical, photocopy, recording, or otherwise, without the prior permission of the publisher, except as provided by USA copyright law.

Scripture quotation (marked MSG) is taken from *THE MESSAGE*, copyright © 1993, 2002, 2018 by Eugene H. Peterson. Used by permission of NavPress. All rights reserved. Represented by Tyndale House Publishers, Inc.

No patent liability is assumed with respect to the use of the information contained herein. Although every precaution has been taken in the preparation of this book, the publisher and author assume no responsibility for errors or omissions. Neither is any liability assumed for damages resulting from the use of the information contained herein.

Published by Maxwell Leadership Publishing, an imprint of Forefront Books, Nashville, Tennessee.
Distributed by Simon & Schuster.

Library of Congress Control Number: 2024904837

Print ISBN: 979-8-88710-039-5
E-book ISBN: 979-8-88710-040-1

Cover Design by Studio Gearbox
Interior Design by PerfecType, Nashville, TN
Printed in the United States of America

*Dedicated to my dad, Lee Gravitt,
who was reliable, generous,
and taught me how to bunt.*

CONTENTS

Introduction   13

PART 1
WINNING BEGINS AT HOME: A STORY

1. *The Request*   19
2. *No Way*   23
3. *Reluctant*   27
4. *Willie*   29
5. *Opening Day*   33
6. *Home*   37
7. *Postgame*   41
8. *Prerequisites*   43
9. *Swing and a Miss*   49
10. *ICU*   55
11. *Love First*   59
12. *Starting Practice*   65
13. *Errors*   69
14. *Home Field Advantage*   75
15. *Bunting*   79
16. *Scoops*   85
17. *Strike Two*   93
18. *Contract Extension*   97
19. *Slumps*   101
20. *A Setback*   105
21. *The Power of a Walk*   109
22. *Winning at Home*   113
23. *Late to Practice*   117
24. *Dinner*   123

PART 2
WINNING BEGINS AT HOME: ACTIVATION GUIDE

Winning Begins at Home Assessment   129
The Prerequisites   133
The Fundamentals   141
Final Challenge   175
Extra Credit   179

Acknowledgments   181
Stay Connected   185
About the Author   187
Notes   191

INTRODUCTION

How amazing would it be if everyone could have a great family? Perhaps the possibility is closer than we think. Admittedly, it is naive to believe the world will suddenly be healed of divisiveness, brokenness, poverty, or evil. As long as there are people, selfishness will continue to turn homes into places filled with shame and blame. But what if . . .? What if real people began to love first and live last?

The story at the core of *Winning Begins at Home* is one born from decades of working with leaders at top businesses, sports teams, and nonprofits. Two tropes have appeared far too often.

The first is the leader who is burning the candle at both ends. They feel like they're constantly at max capacity, overwhelmed, and spread thin, furiously paddling to keep their head above water. The demands at work and home are so tremendous that the stress is keeping either place from receiving the leader's full focus or best efforts.

The second is the leader who is thriving at work and has a prosperous homelife—at least on the surface. Long hours at the office have led to double-digit growth, sales goals blown out of the water, and an enthusiastic, successful team. However, what their colleagues don't see is their struggling homelife, which often includes an empty marriage, health issues, and a consistent track record of missed ballet recitals and weekend soccer tournaments. A family that is getting the *rest* of them, not the *best* of them.

I've found that my personal experiences are aligned with the statistics:

- Two-thirds of US employees are disengaged at work.[1] In other words, the vast majority of people have lost the passion, focus, and devotion to truly succeed on the job.
- When a woman gets promoted, her likelihood of getting a divorce significantly increases.[2]
- The number one cause of stress at home is considered "work" or "money" related, according to the American Psychological Association.[3]
- And, finally, we all know the staggering statistics on divorce—a number that has hovered around 50 percent for years.

INTRODUCTION

WHY NOW?

In the past, there was a clear, often unspoken divide between work life and homelife. In fact, it wasn't until the mid-1980s that the concept of work-life balance even took hold in the United States.

However, with improved technology and more research on the whole person, these worlds have blended; the line between the two, erased. We can't separate who we are from nine to five from who we are from five to nine.

Here's the truth: who we are outside of work is what matters most at work. And who we are at work filters into our homelife, whether we realize it or not.

Never has this become more apparent than right now. As I wrote this book, I reflected on the current state of our world, a few years after the coronavirus pandemic. When the pandemic first began in 2020, many employees were forced to merge their work world and homelife like never before. A 2020 survey of eight hundred human resource executives from across the globe found that 88 percent of organizations encouraged or mandated remote work.[4] The combined effects of families spending more time together during quarantine, marriages being put to the test, and children staying home from school, sports, and activities left a trail of fractured families. Can you relate?

WHY A PARABLE?

After personally coaching and observing hundreds of families for over three decades, I've observed that real people connect with a story more than they do a statistic. We gain hope when we see real people model the right behavior and, maybe more importantly, a warning when others struggle. It reminds us we are not alone. As you read, I'm confident you will see some of yourself in John Williams as he navigates the challenge of loving and leading in the most important place: home. The story that follows is a simple one, but it's not meant to convey that having a healthy family is simple. The fact is, a successful homelife will be one of the most challenging endeavors you will ever sign up for, requiring hard work, humility, sacrifice, and grace. You will fail often, and sometimes badly, but a great family is worth fighting for, and the joy is indescribable when you get it right.

I've always sought to help leaders win, but leaders keep admitting to me that *if you win at work and lose at home, you still lose.* May *Winning Begins at Home* give you a strategy to succeed where it matters most!

| PART ONE |

WINNING BEGINS AT HOME

A STORY

1
The Request

The knock on the front door surprised Kristen Williams. She was having a typical Friday night dinner with her eight-year-old twins, Ella and Emma, and eighteen-month-old daughter, Hannah Kate, who was a surprise two Octobers ago.

The twins jumped up, shouting in unison, "Mom, someone's at the door!"

Precocious Ella followed with, "I'll see who it is."

"Noooo, I'll see who it is," Emma answered, as only an eight-year-old could, as they both sprinted and grabbed the oil-rubbed bronze front doorknob at the same time.

Kristen kept an eye on them as she unbuckled a fussing Hannah Kate from the high chair. The girls welcomed their next-door neighbor, Carol Jackson, into the foyer.

"Come on in, Carol. We were just having dinner," Kristen said, coming to greet her with Hannah Kate on her hip.

"I can come back later. I don't want to interrupt a family dinner."

"It's no problem. It's just the girls and me. John had to work late." John worked late most nights.

"Why don't you finish up and call me when you're through?" Carol's voice and expression were strained.

"Nonsense. Pull up a chair." Kristen led everyone back to the kitchen, nodding to where John should be sitting. "Is everything OK?" she asked as Carol sank into the chair.

"Everything's fine, but I have a request."

"What can we do for you?" Ella asked.

Carol offered a most sincere smile. "Oh, sweet child, just having you next door is more than we deserve." She turned to Kristen. "The request is not really for me; it's actually for Henry."

"What can we do for Mr. Henry?" Emma chimed in, not to be outdone by her twin.

"Is he OK?" Kristen asked, concern in her voice.

"Actually no, he's not doing too well. Henry has been diagnosed with a heart blockage and is going to need surgery next week."

"Oh, I'm so sorry."

"The doctors think he will be fine, but he's going to be down for a few weeks."

THE REQUEST

"How can we help?" Kristen asked.

"Well, you know how Henry coaches Little League baseball. He's been investing in the boys of this community for as long as I can remember. I think John was actually on the very first team Henry coached nearly thirty years ago. Well, anyway, for the past few seasons, Henry has phased into an assistant role. He gave the reins over to Willie Carter. Willie used to play minor league baseball, so Henry says he is better qualified to 'be the skipper,'" Carol quoted with a chuckle.

"Is Daddy going to coach, Mom?" Ella wondered aloud.

"No, sweetie," Kristen answered.

"Actually, we were hoping he would consider it," Carol said with a hint of desperation in her tone.

Knowing her husband would not be interested, nor have the time, Kristen considered her words carefully. But looking at Carol, clearly worried for her husband, she just couldn't find a way to say no. "I'm sure John would love to help. Maybe he can walk over in the morning and Henry can explain what all it entails."

With that, the twins jumped up and down with a, "Wahoo, Daddy is going to be a baseball coach!"

2
No Way

An hour later, the garage door opened when John Williams pressed the small button mounted between the sunroof and windshield of his import sedan. It had been a long week of juggling unsatisfied clients, and he was ready for a couple of days of peace and quiet. Only it wouldn't be quiet. Ella and Emma would see to that.

However, the thought of his twins running to the door to meet him brought a smile to his face as he killed the motor. Kristen would have them bathed and ready for bed, and the smell of fresh shampoo would soon engulf him.

Ella was the first to hear the door. "Daddy's home!" came the shout from upstairs, followed closely by little clean feet running down the hardwood hallway. By the time John set his keys on the counter and peeled off his sport coat, the girls were grabbing each other's arms, enclosing him in their embrace with a big squeeze they referred to as a "daddy sandwich."

"Daddy's home, Daddy's home, Daddy's home," was the unison chant. This nightly ritual was always the highlight of John's day.

Right as Kristen stepped off the last stair with Hannah Kate on her hip, Ella blurted out, "You're coaching baseball, Daddy."

"I'm what?" John glanced at Kristen.

"I'll explain later. Did you have time to—"

"Daddy, come see what I drew in school!" Emma interrupted, tugging on his hand.

"In a minute. Is there anything left to eat?"

"We saved you some pizza. It's in the fridge," Kristen replied.

For the next fifteen minutes, John ate three slices of pepperoni pizza and half listened to the girls tell him about their day at school while Kristen folded laundry upstairs. He was there without really being there. His mind quickly shifted to thoughts of Monday's meeting with a prospective client. He had been working for five months to land the deal, and if it went through, it would add significantly to his income. He wondered if he had prepared enough and decided to put some finishing touches on the presentation over the weekend.

His lack of focus continued as he read an obligatory bedtime story. After the twins finished squabbling over who would sit on which side of him, he made it only a couple of pages in before his mind rushed past the weekend to thoughts of how busy his next week would be.

"What was your favorite part, Daddy?" Emma asked as John turned the final page.

"I liked it all. Now it's time for you girls to get some sleep. Tomorrow is Saturday. You need some rest so we can have a good day."

"Can we go with you to see Mr. Henry about coaching baseball?" Ella pleaded as John reached for the light.

"We'll see," John said as he flipped the switch.

He walked down the hall and met Kristen, who had just put the baby down. "What's this about coaching baseball that Ella keeps talking about?"

She sighed, rubbing her lower back absently and stretching her neck to one side. "Carol stopped by during dinner and shared with us that Henry has a heart blockage. He's going to have a procedure next week and she asked if you'd volunteer with the Little Leaguers as an assistant coach for a few weeks while he recovers. I sort of told her you would."

"No way! How could you? You know I don't have time to coach a bunch of boys right now."

"I know, I'm sorry. It's just Henry needs our help, and they have been such great neighbors to us. Please at least go talk to him in the morning and see what all is involved. If you can't do it, I'm sure he can find someone else."

A coolness hung over the rest of the evening, to say the least. John opened his laptop and brooded to himself, wondering how Kristen could be so unaware of how much pressure he was under. Kristen, meanwhile, sat alone in the family room with a movie playing in the background, exhausted from another week of the monotony of motherhood. Their marriage was far from vibrant, and they both knew it.

3

Reluctant

The next morning, after a pancake breakfast, John reluctantly walked next door to discover Henry Jackson sitting on the front porch holding a double-wall mug of piping-hot coffee while reading the paper.

"Good morning, Coach." The fact John still called Henry "Coach" after nearly thirty years was a tribute to the contribution Henry had made in his life as a ten-year-old.

"John! How are you, neighbor?" His hearty reply came from behind the sports section.

"I'm OK. How are you? That's the better question. Kristen tells me your ticker is acting up."

Folding the paper, Henry answered, "Oh, just a little minor procedure. No need to worry. The doc says I'll feel twenty years younger after he cleans everything out."

"I hear you're going to be down a few weeks with your recovery, and you're looking for a baseball coach."

"That's right. You interested? The pay's not very good, but I don't suppose that matters. I hear your consulting business is going well."

"Listen, Coach, I'm awfully busy, and I have never coached boys. The closest thing on my résumé is one year of six-year-old-girls soccer. That's a lot different than Little League baseball."

"The guys really could use your help, John. They're just kids, the same as girls, and Willie will do all the heavy lifting. I just need a pinch hitter for four weeks, and then I'll be back. An hour-long practice on Tuesday nights and a game on Saturday mornings. So what do you say?"

Walking back across the yard, John mumbled to himself his disbelief that he had agreed, but he knew it was the right thing to do. Coach Henry had volunteered as a coach for three decades. John had calculated the total hours for four Tuesday practices and the ninety-minute games on Saturdays and figured the least he could do was give ten hours.

Four weeks, he thought to himself. *You can handle four weeks, and then you're done.*

4
Willie

On Tuesday at 6:59 p.m., John's car rocked to a stop at the Riverside Recreation Center. He had grabbed takeout on the way and was finishing the last bite of cheeseburger as he slammed the gear in Park.

On field three, he found a group of a dozen boys playing toss in groups of two. He recognized the lean, athletic Willie Carter lining bats up near the on-deck circle.

Willie, now in his midfifties, looked like he could still play at the highest level. After retiring from baseball at twenty-nine, never having made it to the big leagues, Willie had returned to Riverside and gone to work in construction. A decade later, he had started his own company and made it big as a real estate developer. With the recent sale of the business, Willie was officially retired, much to the admiration of the community. He had done things the right way and was now positioned to give back to the next generation through his coaching and private hitting lessons.

"Coach Carter, I'm John Williams. I believe Coach Henry told you I would be taking his place while he is laid up for a few weeks."

"I'm afraid no one could take Henry's place," Willie said with a smile.

"There is no doubt about that," John said admiringly of his old coach as he reached to shake Willie's hand.

"Welcome to the team," Willie stated with strength in his voice.

Over the next hour, John was mesmerized with how organized and efficient Willie ran things. John mostly stood around observing, but he did prove helpful near the end of practice hitting pop flies to the outfielders while Willie worked with the infielders. When it was over, the boys bagged up the equipment as Willie and John walked out to the parking lot. In the cab of his truck, Willie had a team cap with a Rangers logo and the game schedule for John. Handing him both, he dropped the tailgate and asked John to sit for a minute.

"So tell me a little bit about yourself," Willie invited.

"Not much to tell, I guess. I run a consulting company. I'm married, with eight-year-old twin girls, Ella and Emma, and an eighteen-month-old baby, Hannah Kate. I've never coached baseball, but I did play through high school. I was actually on Coach Henry's first Little

League team on this very field twenty-eight years ago. It was the year they built the rec center. You were playing in the Orioles farm system and every kid around here wanted to be you. Seems like a lifetime ago."

Willie laughed as he reminisced about his own Little League days. "Back when I was growing up, we had only one field. It was down by Riverside Park. It didn't even have a fence in the outfield."

"I played T-ball on that field," John said.

"Henry tells me your business is crushing it. Sounds like you have a great life both at work and at home."

"I guess," John agreed, trying to convince himself.

Picking up on a hint of doubt, Willie quizzed, "You don't sound so sure."

Maybe it was the fact that Willie asked with no judgment in his tone or that he was the one who appeared to have it all together. John had heard what a great family man Willie was. Word around town was he cared more about success off the field than he did on it. John wasn't sure what that meant, but Henry had told him Willie was someone he could learn from. Whatever the reason, over the next half hour, John opened up and admitted things were better on the surface than they were in reality. He revealed he was overwhelmed by the demands on his time and the complexity of the changing business climate. He acknowledged he often felt like the bottleneck to a company that was ready to be scaled. While he didn't reveal it to Willie, John knew his homelife was no better. He sensed he was losing there too.

Willie was a good listener. When the conversation finally wound down, he said, "Well, I'm glad you're a part of the team. Thanks for being so honest with your story. I really look forward to becoming friends over the next few weeks. Now, we better send you home before you get in trouble with all those girls you live with." The two men laughed together as they parted ways.

On the drive home, John could not believe he had been so vulnerable with a complete stranger. Yet in his heart he felt somehow relieved. It was the first time he had opened up to anyone in several years. He and Kristen used to have long, enjoyable talks, but for the last couple of years the conversations had dwindled to texts about mealtime schedules and occasional small talk before bed. As he turned in the driveway and faced his truth, he felt like a lousy husband and father.

Home, once his favorite place, now lacked hope. He could feel his family slipping away, much like a home team's chance of victory when trailing in the bottom of the ninth. If something didn't change, it might be game over for the Williams family.

5
Opening Day

On Saturday morning, the skies over the ballpark were gloomy, but the rain held off, much to the excitement of the Riverside Rangers and the neighboring Madison Marlins. It was opening day, and despite the cool temperature, parents and grandparents filled the stands to watch their little guys play.

The hometown Rangers scored a run when they batted in the first inning but fell behind 1–2 in the second. The day looked hopeless when the Marlins' cleanup hitter, Charlie Cook, jacked a grand slam in the top of the third, pushing the deficit to 1–6.

"That kid looks like he's in high school," John remarked to Willie as Cook rounded third.

"Bigger than most of the guys in the minors, back in the day," Willie agreed with a laugh.

The Rangers gained ground, cutting it to 3–6 with two runs in the bottom of the third and had a chance to tie in the fourth when the first two hitters settled for walks, bringing the Rangers slugger, Drew Duncan, to the plate.

John was surprised when Willie signaled for Drew to bunt in order to move the runners over to second and third. Duncan laid one down perfectly along the first base line, and both runners advanced. A subsequent sacrifice fly led to a single run, tightening the score to 4–6 heading to the fifth.

The Rangers pitchers were brilliant the last couple of innings, holding the Marlins scoreless. And the hitters were just as good, pushing across two more runs in the fifth.

And then a game winner in the bottom of the sixth when the speedy Timmy Turner stole home. The crowd went wild with the 7–6 victory.

After the game, Willie gathered the boys and congratulated them on the win. "You guys executed the strategy perfectly. I'm so proud of you. Enjoy the weekend and we will see you at practice Tuesday night."

As the boys dispersed, John caught Willie's attention. "Can I ask you a question?"

"Sure. Fire away."

"Why did you have Duncan bunt in the fourth when we had a chance to tie the game?"

"That's a fair question. It was a tough decision, but it's what our strategy called for."

"We had a strategy?"

"That's right."

"I didn't realize a strategy was needed for ten- to twelve-year-olds."

"A strategy is needed anytime you compete," Willie answered. "And the rule of seven rarely lets us down."

"What's the rule of seven?"

"John, I started coaching in this league nine years ago. The first two years I helped Henry as an assistant. He and I both loved investing in the boys, and we also loved to compete. But not just compete; we loved to win. So we did a bit of research and discovered that anytime a team in this age group scores seven runs in a game, the probability of winning is 92 percent. Those are pretty good odds in any endeavor, much less baseball. Over the past decade the numbers have barely changed. Seven runs still wins 90 percent of the time. When Drew came to bat in the fourth, I wasn't interested in getting to six, I was building toward seven. Six wouldn't have been enough. And besides, the probability of him hitting a home run was very low. He more likely would have struck out had he been trying to tie the game. Homers are sporadic. I'm more interested in strategic."

"That's interesting," John acknowledged.

"Think about your business. As the leader, would you ever go into a fiscal year without a strategic plan?" Willie continued.

"I guess not," John replied, knowing there were many areas where he was winging it at work. He hadn't felt like much of a leader lately.

"You guess not?" Willie challenged him. "You better not if you hope to win."

"We have a strategic plan," John quickly assured.

"Most leaders start with a plan and even review it and work accordingly. But unfortunately, when a crisis pops up the plan goes out the window, and many leaders begin to react sporadically rather than strategically."

"Guilty as charged, I guess." John grinned.

"The question isn't, *Do you have a plan?* but, *Are you willing to stick to the plan when tempted to veer off course?* Think about it; do you know how hard it was to ask our best hitter to bunt with two men on base, knowing his parents, as well as everyone else watching, was questioning me, including you?" Willie smiled wryly.

"Pretty hard, I'm guessing."

"You need to stop all this guessing. It was very hard. Without our rule of seven strategy, I would have caved, and chances are we would have lost the game."

John took it all in with the realization his business plan was much more sporadic than it was strategic.

"Home is no different." Willie's words interrupted John's train of thought. "You need a strategy there too, if you intend to win," Willie said confidently.

"A strategy for home?"

As they walked toward the gate, Willie paused on home plate and raked the dust off with his left foot. "John, just like in baseball, winning begins at home."

6

Home

After his postgame conversation with Willie, John's head spun with the phrase "winning begins at home." If that were true, he was striking out as a husband and father. Four months earlier, John had arrived home, late as usual, to find Kristen on the back deck with both hands wrapped around a cup of coffee as if clinging to hope. Her words, *"John, we need help. I can't go on like this... We can't go on like this,"* had rocked his world.

For the next twenty-five minutes, Kristen had spilled her guts about feeling neglected by him, overwhelmed by motherhood, and afraid of what the future might hold. There had been desperation in her tone. Though she didn't raise her voice, or even attack, she clearly sounded resigned to their fate. The words were stunning. John knew things were bad, but he had no idea how bad. All of a sudden, their marriage felt like a derailed train heading for peril. *Were things really about to end?* he had wondered. He felt bad for Kristen, but what could he do to help? He didn't know the answer, and even if he did, he was equally overwhelmed at work, and no one was coming to his rescue. He knew he should say something affirming, but words failed him. For the next few weeks, things remained icy as the two of them labored through a silent separation. Recently, things had stabilized, maybe even slightly improved, but they were still nowhere near where they needed to be.

Truthfully, home had become an endless string of mundane moments. To those looking from the outside, he and Kristen had a great marriage, three adorable girls, and a dream life. Yet, on the inside, they had both lost perspective and things were crumbling.

Before kids, Kristen had been a nurse in the Riverside Regional ER. The two of them had met when John broke his collarbone playing touch football with his brothers and their buddies on Thanksgiving Day. Kristen had reluctantly given him her number.

After turning him down a couple of times, she eventually agreed to a date. Six months later they were engaged. Kristen intended to continue her career after the pregnancy, but once they discovered twins were on the way, staying home with the girls became the best option. She had no regrets.

John had grown up in Riverside and, upon graduating from the University of North Carolina, returned after landing a marketing job with a local start-up focused on innovation. His creativity had accelerated his growth, and by thirty he branched out and started his own consulting firm. Within two years, his business exploded. John couldn't hire people fast enough to meet the growing demands of his customers. The business required most of his time, and Kristen and the girls took a back seat.

While John was winning from nine to five, he had never really considered that what happens from five to nine was equally, if not more, important.

7
Postgame

As John walked in the door after Saturday's game, Kristen's greeting, "That was a great game," were her first positive words to John in a long time. Feeling guilty for lassoing John into coaching, she had loaded up the girls and driven to the ballpark to watch.

"Yeah, it was a nail-biter. Thanks for bringing the girls. Did they have fun?"

"They did. On the way home they both said they want to play baseball next year." The two of them shared a rare laugh.

"Listen, I think it's great you're helping out Henry," Kristen said.

"It's not like I had much choice," he quickly reminded her with a hint of frustration.

"Look, I'm sorry. I thought you would enjoy doing something other than work for a change."

"Why do you always have to complain about my work? My job is what allows you to stay home and be with the girls."

"I'm not complaining. We only wish you were around more."

Deep in his heart, John knew she was right. The business gave him a place to avoid the strain he felt with Kristen and the girls, so he worked even more.

"I guess it was good being out there with the guys," he admitted.

"I'm sure Henry appreciates it too," Kristen said.

Three more weeks and Coach Henry will return and I can get back to my life, he thought. Only it didn't feel like much of a life. John knew his family was hanging by a thread. He and Kristen's communication was nonexistent, he was missing important moments with his girls, and he was becoming more and more detached.

John spent the rest of the weekend catching up on paperwork and working in the yard. Willie's words constantly crossed his mind . . . *winning begins at home*. He didn't fully comprehend why he was struggling but suspected if he could not figure things out at home, winning at work wouldn't matter.

8
Prerequisites

By Tuesday morning, John found himself neck-deep in another busy week. When his four o'clock appointment canceled, he oddly felt glad and found himself looking forward to baseball practice. John atypically ended his day an hour early and stopped by the house for dinner with Kristen and the kids. After the meal he grabbed his Rangers cap, kissed the girls, and headed to the field.

Arriving forty-five minutes early, he found Willie already on the field, preparing for practice. The two of them set out the bases and started raking the infield.

As they groomed the dirt together, the two coaches eased back into their conversation from the previous week.

"How was your weekend, John?"

"The weekend was fine. Kristen brought the twins to the game and now they both want to play baseball next year," John replied with a laugh.

"It was a pretty exciting game, wasn't it?" Willie chuckled.

"It really was, and I must give you props for your rule of seven strategy."

"Thanks, but I can't take much credit. The numbers sort of took all the guessing out of the equation. All I had to do was stick to the plan."

"Can I ask you about something you said after the game? I've been thinking about it all weekend. The whole 'winning begins at home' thing—I was curious what you meant by having a strategy."

"That's a fair question, I guess," Willie replied.

"I thought we weren't supposed to be guessing," John needled back without looking up from his raking.

Willie grinned. "I hear ya." He continued, "When it comes to a strategy for winning at home, I like to keep it simple. At home, seven is too many. There, I only have a rule of two."

"This ought to be good. Let's hear it."

"First let me give you two prerequisites. You might call these the 'pregame talk.'"

"Sounds complicated—more like a rule of four," John challenged.

Willie gave a long pull on the rake. "I'll go slow. I think you can handle it. And actually, it used to be only the rule of two. I added the two prerequisites because they make it easier to stick to the strategy. You might say they are like the leadoff man in baseball."

"The leadoff man?"

"Yeah. The percentages go way up that runs will be scored when the leadoff hitter reaches base in an inning. In the same way, whenever these two prerequisites are in place, it's like having men on base."

"Makes sense," John agreed.

"OK, let me start with a question. What kind of family do you want?"

John stood up straight and paused. "Excuse me?"

"What kind of family do you want? It's not a hard question."

"A good one, I guess. I mean, I know," he corrected himself before Willie could bust him for guessing. "A good one."

"Is that it?" Willie pushed. "What do you mean? Is that all you want to be able to say? I have a good family."

"Well, no, I'm sure there's more than that."

"Like what?"

"Like, I guess for us to all get along and enjoy being a family. And I wish Kristen and I would love each other the way we used to. I also hope we can provide so the girls can have things better than we had them. Things like that."

"What if I told you that you could lay down all of your guessing and wishing and hoping? That you could actually define what kind of family you want, and there is a strategy to help you have it?"

"I'd say I want to hear about it."

"We'll get to it. But first, I want you to spend some time defining what kind of family you want to have. There's no one way to do that. For me, I asked myself questions. *What kind of relationship do I want to have with my wife? What do I want our communication and our connection to feel like? What kind of father do I want to be? What kind of children do we hope to raise? How do I want the people in my home to feel about me?*"

"I honestly haven't given those questions much thought," John admitted.

"Sadly, most people don't," Willie said. "I spent years in the construction business and it was amazing how many people asked me to build them a house without thinking about what they really wanted. I learned there's a difference in a generic set of drawings and a custom blueprint. The families with a blueprint ended up with the nicest homes. If I can be blunt, what you describe sounds more like a spec home than a dream home."

Willie's words were pointed, yet they didn't feel judgmental. And John knew he was right.

"The place to start," Willie said before John could ask, "is what I call prerequisite one: **define what kind of family you want**."

John nodded. "I'll give it more thought. What's the second prerequisite?"

Willie glanced to where the boys were arriving and already starting to warm up in the outfield. John followed his gaze, admiring the smooth infield beneath the dusty practice bases, thinking how Willie must have done the same thousands of times during his playing days.

"Let's save number two until after practice, if you have a few minutes to stick around," Willie said. Then he yelled for the boys to come and circle up.

"Sounds good," John agreed as the kids sprinted from the outfield grass toward the coaches.

The next hour passed quickly as the Little Leaguers practiced the fundamentals of fielding and each took a turn at the plate with Willie pitching. John spent most of the hour pondering the question, *What kind of family do I want?* He knew he needed to give it more thought and maybe even discuss it with Kristen. But one thing was for sure, his answer would likely reveal a gap between his vision and his current reality.

When practice was over, once again the two new friends sat on Willie's tailgate and debriefed the practice. Within moments Willie stood up and said, "I want to leave you with one more thing to think about between now and Saturday."

"Is it prerequisite number two?" John asked.

"It is," Willie acknowledged.

"OK. Let's have it."

"Decide why."

"Decide why, what?" John asked, a bit confused.

"**Decide why you want to have a family**. What is your motivation? If you can define what kind of family you want and decide why you want to have a family, you will be perfectly positioned to win at home."

"Can you say more about 'decide why'?" John asked.

Willie lowered himself off the tailgate and walked around to the driver's door. John closed the tailgate and followed.

"I really can't," Willie said as he climbed in. "Only you can define what and decide why. It's your family. I can tell you this, though: if you can't answer both, you will always struggle. But if you can wrestle your vision and your motive to the ground, you really can have an amazing family. Call me if I can help."

With those words Willie put his big truck into Drive and let off the brake.

As the diesel came to life and rolled away, John realized he had work to do and some very important questions to answer.

Define what and decide why rolled over in his mind again and again as he made the short drive home. He arrived in time to tuck in the girls. Then, excited to make progress, he retired to his home office, took out a legal pad, wrote *Williams Family Blueprint* across the top of the page, and made two columns, *Define What* and *Decide Why*. When he finally fell into bed, Kristen, exhausted from the day, was already in a deep sleep. Sensing he should have her weigh in on the blueprint, he was tempted to wake her but thought better of it. It could wait until morning.

9
Swing and a Miss

The next morning John showered, dressed, and buzzed into the kitchen to find Ella feeding Cheerios to Hannah Kate, one at a time, with her fingers.

"Where's your mom?" he asked.

"Her and Emma went to the store. We're out of coffee and she'll be right back so you can fill up your mug."

"I can't wait, sweetie. Let me see if Mrs. Jackson is next door and can watch you two for a few minutes."

After a quick call to Carol confirmed she would be right over, John kissed both girls on the forehead, told Ella Mrs. Jackson would be here any second, and Mom would be back soon.

"OK, Daddy," Ella replied.

Hannah Kate gave her best "Da Da Da Da" as John rushed out the door. He texted Kristen as he hit the Start button on the car:

Sorry I missed you. Running late. Carol is watching the girls. See you at dinner.

Kristen was on the coffee aisle when her phone buzzed. Furious after reading the text, she didn't bother to answer. How could he leave the girls alone and not wait on her? Did he not recognize the last thing she wanted to be doing was grocery shopping this early in the morning? She was doing it for him, and he didn't even have the awareness to be appreciative.

John drove straight to a Starbucks three blocks from his office and ordered a venti Americana. The drive-through was packed with cars. As he waited in line, he felt a wave of frustration, *How hard is it to make sure there's coffee in the house?*

Once he had his drink in hand, John decided to call Willie and tell him about his progress on the blueprint. After all, Willie had said to call, and John wanted to make sure he was on the right track.

Willie answered on the second ring with a bold, "Need help already?"

"Good morning to you too."

"How is it out there in the working world today?" Willie inquired with a hint of retired happiness in his voice.

"Low on coffee."

"That's a shame, but I'm guessing that's not why you called. What can I do for you?"

"Well, you said to reach out if I needed help, and I wanted to let you know I worked on my blueprint last night. Wanted to see if you think I'm on the right track."

"That's great, let's hear what you have," Willie said.

"OK, you said simple is good. Here's what I wrote. 'I want a family where we love each other completely, no matter what.'"

"That sounds like a great family. Is that it?"

"No, there's one more thing. 'I want us to like each other as much as we love each other.'"

Willie laughed and replied, "Now that sounds like a really great family. That's super, John. It appears you have defined what kind of family you want. Your definition may be refined or tweaked as you go, but I think you'll find the idea of a home full of love where people like each other through the ups and downs to be a good starting point. Tell me why you want to have this lovable, likable home."

"Well, I started thinking, and it feels like there would be a lot more joy, and it would be less stressful if those things were true."

"Joy and fun are a great why. Anything else?"

"Actually, there is. I suppose if we're struggling, there must be other families that aren't perfect either. It seems impossible, but maybe our family could be an encouragement to others who want to make progress."

"That's great, John. What did Kristen have to say about all of this?"

"Actually, I didn't run it by her yet."

"What? Why not?"

"Well, after the kids went down last night, I went into my office and started working on this, and she was already asleep when I finished. This morning she made a coffee run before I saw her and we just missed each other."

"I'm sorry to hear it. Do you think the last twelve hours reflected what you wrote on your blueprint?"

"Not really. I guess I sort of messed up."

"No, you really messed up. A swing and a miss, my friend. But there is hope for you yet. You just need a strategy."

"It's about time," John jabbed back.

"Do you have plans for lunch tomorrow?"

"I can probably push a couple of things. What did you have in mind?"

"A strategy session. Meet me at Riverside Regional. I'll be at the elevators in the lobby at 11:45," Willie said and clicked off the call.

When John got home that night, an angry Kristen met him at the door.

"How could you?" She didn't give him a chance to respond. She stormed back into the kitchen to finish making dinner. Those were the only words she said to him the entire night.

Recognizing the weight of his insensitivity, John knew better than to defend himself. *How could I be such an idiot?*

The silence of the adults rang louder than the noise of the kids. Morning couldn't come soon enough.

10
ICU

The next day, John parked his car in visitor parking, wondering what the heck he was doing at the hospital. Since spending a week inside as a kid with a blood infection, he hadn't wanted to have anything to do with doctors. The only three times he had been back were when he broke his collarbone, when the twins were born, and when Hannah Kate came along.

He walked through a big glass atrium and spotted a receptionist sitting behind a massive semicircle desk. Over her left shoulder was a wall of four elevators and Willie standing there with a big smile on his face.

John quickly walked around the receptionist, who was on the phone, and strode up to his new friend.

"Good morning, John."

"Good morning. I have to ask: What in the world are we doing in a hospital?"

"I was expecting that question. Come with me." Willie punched the up arrow with his left index finger.

The elevator doors opened and the two men entered, joining three nurses who were evidently on their way back up from the cafeteria.

They exchanged greetings as Willie touched the 3 on the panel. Beside the button, John noticed the words *ICU Waiting*. Within seconds, the doors opened and Willie exited, leaving John standing with the nurses who were headed up to the fourth floor. John barely beat the doors as he hopped out into the corridor. Willie was already fifteen feet down the hall to the right, his long stride leaving John behind. Willie turned into a room seven doors down on the left under a sign that read "Waiting Room."

By the time John reached the door, Willie had found a seat in the far corner of the large area that was full of nearly two dozen people who were clustered in little groups of two to five people. Each pod looked like a campsite, with blankets, pillows, bags of snacks, and laptops. There were phone and computer chargers plugged into every outlet around the room.

Willie motioned for John, who was standing in the doorway taking it all in, to come over and join him.

"You didn't answer my question," John whispered as he sat in the chair on Willie's right.

"Welcome to How to Have a Great Family 101," Willie replied, picking up on John's curiosity as to why they were there.

"I don't understand."

"Remember how I told you we were going to have a strategy session?"

"Yes."

"I know this might feel odd, but I want you to sit here for ten minutes with me and simply observe what happens in this room. Will you do that for me? Take note of what you see, hear, and feel."

John thought to himself, *Either this guy is crazy or I'm losing it, big time*, but nodded as he looked around the space.

He first locked in on a young man who was sitting with a woman and two young boys. The oldest appeared to be a tad younger than Ella and Emma. Unbeknownst to John, the couple's teen daughter had been in a car accident and was lying on the other side of the waiting room wall in a coma with a severe head injury. John was mesmerized as he observed the older of the two boys reading a children's book to the younger. Big brother patiently encouraged his sibling to turn the page each time they reached the end. John couldn't fathom the twins reading quietly together. The father of the family stood to make a coffee run. He stopped to ask the family in the adjacent pod what he could bring them. Within minutes he was back with a drink holder full of piping-hot coffee, exactly as each person had requested.

On the far side of the room a doctor stood blocking from John's sight two young men who appeared to be about his age. Their mom was having a kidney transplant and apparently the news was good. At least judging from the intensity of the way they simultaneously hugged the doctor, laughing through their tears.

There were two elderly women, one Black and one White, who sat reminiscing about their grandchildren. Both of their husbands had had heart bypass surgery the day before and were still in ICU.

A couple was camped in the corner with a small girl, maybe three years old. The dad had built a small fort over three wooden chairs using a bedsheet. The little girl was sitting in her mom's lap, holding a baby doll. Dad looked to be praying with his face buried in his hands. Mom had one arm wrapped around the little girl and the other hand on the dad's shoulder.

The entire room was a picture of love. John could literally feel it. He knew all of these people were hurting and yet here they all sat, serving one another, sharing stories, and all silently wishing miracles on complete strangers.

John looked over at Willie, who was looking at him. Willie whispered, "Seen enough?"

John nodded as Willie patted him on the shoulder and said, "Come with me."

The two men went back out the same way they had come in. When they reached the atrium, instead of heading to the entrance, Willie veered off toward two comfortable chairs cornered by a bank of windows. John was ready to hear the first two words that would alter his home forever.

11
Love First

As the two men sat together, Willie asked John what he had noticed. John recalled each scenario in his mind before blurting out a single word. "Love."

This brought a smile to Willie's face. "It was obvious, wasn't it?"

"It really was," John replied.

Leaning forward in his chair, Willie said, "There may be no better place on the planet to see what love looks like than an ICU waiting room. When my mother-in-law died a few years back, we spent several days in a room like the one we just left. I couldn't help but notice how kind everyone was. People served each other, prayed together, cheered for each other, shared hugs as needed, and believed the best even when things were hopeless. There was no prejudice. Color didn't matter. No socio-economic classes. No one had an agenda other than seeing their loved one well again. It got me to thinking, John. What if home was that kind of place?"

"That would be pretty cool," John responded.

"Wouldn't it, though? So here's the real question. Is that what your home looks and feels like?"

Willie's words pierced John because the truth was, he had been more self-serving than serving. In fact, his selfishness seemed to be fracturing their lives. There was very little patience, kindness, or encouragement in their communication.

Somehow despair had replaced joy. Love was definitely not ruling the day. "I'm afraid not," John admitted.

"I know how you feel, buddy. There was a time when my home was a mess too."

"Really? I thought things were pretty great for you; at least that's what Henry told me."

"Actually they're pretty great now," Willie said with a smile.

"How did you move from a mess to where you are today?" John asked with a hint of hope.

"I learned about love as a strategy."

"Love as a strategy?"

"Well, let me be clear. Love is not a strategy. Love is love. If it becomes a strategy, it is no longer love. That said, there is nothing that will help you win at home more than **love first**."

"Love first?"

"Love first," Willie affirmed.

"Some people are hard to love. I mean, I love Kristen, but I'm just not feeling in love like I used to. And to be honest, I'm not feeling the love from her either. Some of the stuff she says or does—or doesn't do. Sometimes our marriage is a mess."

"Don't be confused. *Love* is not just a noun. *Love* is also a verb. Love covers up a mess. It gives the benefit of the doubt. It wants what is best for the other person. It is considerate, kind, resilient, patient, and thoughtful. John, *love* is the most powerful word in the history of the world."

"But you said love is a strategy and then you said it isn't. Either it is or it isn't."

"That's the crazy part. Remember when I said one of the prerequisites was to know your why? Love requires the right motivation, or it ceases to be love. If I love only based on how it benefits me, I miss the mark and mess it up. But I promise, if you can get it right and truly love first, it's like a miracle cure for everything else. If you really want to win at home, start with love."

"Sometimes it's hard to love first at my house."

"That's what my wife says too," Willie agreed with a chuckle.

"Seriously, Kristen and I both have our flaws."

"We all do. But love is a choice. You get to decide whether you want to focus on the flaws or look for what is good. From my own experience, when I focus on what is wrong, I usually find it really quick, and I have a tendency to be harsh with people, or at least I used to. I finally learned that intensity can kill intimacy."

"Ouch!"

"When I was playing ball, we had a chaplain who came and spoke to our team at a series on the West Coast. I remember him saying, *'You're never persuasive when you're abrasive.'* Those words busted me between the eyes, and I've never forgotten. The truth was, whenever my wife, Karen, made the slightest mistake, I was quick to point it out. There were times when I was harsh and even raised my voice toward the woman I loved the most, hoping to make my point. All I did was hurt her, though. And saying something louder doesn't make me more right or the one on the receiving end motivated to change."

John sat there taking it all in, knowing he was guilty of everything Willie was describing. For the past several months, he had escalated arguments with Kristen when he didn't like how she did something, and he had chosen to hold on to anger for days at a time. He also knew he had been too hard on Ella when she was loud or challenged him or Kristen. His mind was swirling with remorse.

Gathering himself, John asked, "Who taught you all of this, Willie?"

"Love did."

"Love?"

"John, I've been married for over thirty years. You don't make it that long because you picked the perfect person. In fact, there are no perfect people."

"That's a fact," John agreed.

Willie continued, "Marriage is the greatest classroom on the planet to learn about sacrifice, and love has been my teacher. Love—real love—has held Karen and me together. Without love saving the day over and over, we would have split up years ago."

Those last words jolted John. He didn't want to think about him and Kristen splitting up, but he also knew they couldn't stay the current course. They didn't have a love-first home. Love felt like an afterthought.

"Willie, why are you sharing this with me?"

"Because I want you to have a great family, and I believe you can. I actually want everyone to be a part of a great family. There's nothing better in the world than a home full of love, and nothing much harder than one filled with strife. Everyone needs to love and be loved—to win at home."

"Thanks. It's funny, I thought I was helping out Coach Henry. It turns out I may be the one who needed the most help."

Willie stood, slapped John on the back, and said, "I'll see you Saturday. In the meantime, go home and practice."

12

Starting Practice

John spent the rest of the afternoon half present at work. After sitting through a couple of meetings and reviewing the quarterly financials, he decided to go home and get to the real work of trying to improve his family.

Kristen was surprised to see him so early, but not nearly as surprised as she was to find him holding a bouquet of cut flowers when he walked through the door.

"I love you," were the first words out of his mouth when he walked in the kitchen. "I know those words are hollow and I need to show it with my actions, but I wanted you to know, I still love you and I'm sorry things have been so rocky."

Tears welled up in Kristen's eyes as she raised her hand to her mouth and blurted out, "Are you having an affair?"

"No, I'm not having an affair! Are you nuts!? I'm trying to say I'm sorry."

"What are you sorry for, Daddy?" Ella asked as she rounded the corner into the kitchen.

On her heels was Emma, who followed with, "Did you bring us flowers, Daddy?"

John knelt and looked Emma in the eyes. "No, sweetie, the flowers are for Mommy."

Both girls giggled and looked up at Kristen, who was smiling through her tears.

"Why don't you guys go grab a soccer ball and meet me in the backyard? Hannah Kate and I are looking for a game of two-on-two if you girls are up for it."

"Hannah Kate doesn't play soccer. She's a baby," Ella said, rolling her eyes.

"You let me worry about that. Now go find a ball and meet me in five minutes."

Emma said, "Bet I can find it first!" and the kitchen was once again clear of kids.

John looked back at Kristen, handed her the flowers, and reiterated, "Look, I know I haven't shown it much lately, but I really do love you, and I want us to have a great family. We can talk more about it later, but right now I want you to have the next couple of hours off. I'm going to hang out with the girls. You can grab a book, go hit the gym, take a walk, or anything else you want to do. We will even take care of dinner and have something ready at seven. Now go enjoy the rest of your afternoon."

Kristen stood there stunned. As John turned to go change out of his work clothes, Hannah Kate came toddling down the hall babbling, "Da Da Da Da."

"Let's go play some soccer, baby girl," John said as he scooped her up in his arms and headed upstairs. He stopped by the twins' room and asked them to keep an eye on the baby while he went back down and put on some shorts.

Five minutes later they were all running through the backyard. Hannah Kate squealed with delight as John carried her around on his shoulders while Emma and Ella played keep-away from him. It was all smiles until John scolded Ella.

"Easy, Ella. You're playing way too rough!"

Ella's smile melted from her face more quickly than the sweat droplets fell from her reddened cheeks. Her head dropped and her gaze pointed toward her grass-stained knees, but not before John could see the tears well up. His words weren't abrasive, but they definitely were deflating. Truthfully, Emma was being just as aggressive, but Ella, being the loudest, was typically held to a higher standard. Before John recognized his double standard, Ella sprinted toward the back patio.

"Ella, stop, I was just—" But she didn't slow down.

Emma stood silently as Hannah Kate cooed with confusion.

John muttered to himself, "This love-first stuff is going to be harder than I thought."

Rather than doing something to replenish herself, Kristen simply sat in the parking lot at a local coffee shop and closed her eyes. She thought of how everything at home was resting on her shoulders. She felt the burden of keeping everyone fed, helping with homework, managing chores, and John's lack of awareness—especially John's lack of awareness. *A two-hour break isn't going to solve everything* was her last thought before she drifted off to sleep.

By the time she awakened and returned, dinner was long over. John had made things right with Ella and had everyone ready for bed. Expecting Kristen to be rejuvenated, he was a bit frustrated when she failed to say thank you for the break and apologize for missing dinner. Wasn't she grateful? Didn't she appreciate all he was doing for the family by working so hard?

They clearly weren't on the same page. Rather than ask her how she was doing and discussing how he was feeling, the two of them went to bed. Another opportunity missed for John to really connect with Kristen.

13

Errors

On Saturday, the Rangers traveled to Centerville to face the Braves in a highly anticipated clash of undefeated teams. Things fell apart in the second inning when Riverside's shortstop, Cole Palmer, made three consecutive throwing errors. Cole was the best player on the team, but today he looked like he had never seen a baseball, much less thrown one. As the third one sailed wide right and into the first base dugout, two more Braves scored, giving Centerville a three-run lead. Palmer dropped his head in shame. Willie called time-out and headed to the mound. The Riverside infielders huddled around him.

Inside the huddle, Willie put his arm around Cole and began whispering something in his ear no one else could hear. Cole looked up into Coach Willie's eyes and said, "Yes, sir."

Like the previous week, the Rangers rallied, scoring four runs during the middle innings, eventually taking a one-run lead. As the teams reached the bottom of the last inning, Centerville had three outs to determine who would leave undefeated.

After walking the first three batters to load the bases, the Rangers finally recorded a strikeout to secure the first out. With the bases loaded, Centerville sent their own shortstop to the plate with the game on the line. The first two pitches were a little low, causing the tension in the ballpark to rise. The Centerville fans screamed for a hit.

A fastball sped right down the middle, leading to the crack of the bat. The ball went speeding into the gap between shortstop and third base. Cole dove to his right, grabbed the hard grounder with his glove, and fired a strike to Timmy Turner, who was playing second base. Timmy caught the ball, quickly avoided the sliding runner, and threw the ball with all his might toward first base. The ball beat the Centerville shortstop by a half step, resulting in an unbelievable double play. Game over . . . another Rangers win! The entire team mobbed Cole, and the celebration was on.

The trip back to Riverside was boisterous as the players recalled the highlights of the triumph. When the ride was over, the boys filed off the bus. John noticed Willie walk Cole out to where his mom was waiting in the parking lot. As Cole climbed into the back seat with his little brother, Willie leaned down at the driver's window, patted Miss Palmer on the arm, and proceeded to describe in detail how Cole had overcome adversity and made the play of the day to end the game.

"You should be proud of this kid," Willie affirmed, looking into the back seat and winking at Cole.

Cole beamed as his mom smiled with pride.

"Thank you for coaching. He loves being on your team," she replied.

"We'll see you Tuesday. Work hard in school this week, Cole."

"Yes, sir."

As the car shifted into Reverse and backed out of the spot, Willie turned back to John, who had wandered over toward the conversation.

"Cole's mom?"

"Miss Palmer."

"Why didn't she come to the game?"

"She's a single mom and works on Saturdays at Riverside Dry Cleaners across town. She rarely makes it to away games, but she does what she can. She's a good mom. Her boys are fortunate to have her."

"Cole has brothers?"

"Yeah, two. One is seven and one is four," Willie answered.

"How do you know them so well?"

"I know all of the families on our team. It's hard to love the players if you don't really know them."

"Love the players?" John asked.

"Yeah. Why do you think I do this?"

"I guess I hadn't really thought about it."

"You don't need to guess this time. I'm doing this for the kids. I really do love them. If it was about me, I'd be fishing this afternoon. There's certainly no Hall of Fame for Little League managers, even if they go undefeated," Willie said with a big grin.

"Can I ask you something?"

"You bet. Anything."

"What did you whisper to Cole on your visit to the mound?"

"I told him I loved him, and I believed in him, and that if he threw every single ball for the rest of the season into the dugout, I would still want him to be my shortstop. Then I asked him if he believed me. He said, 'Yes, sir,' and that was all I needed to hear."

"That's awesome!"

"After the inning, when Cole came back to the dugout, he thanked me for encouraging him. I told him not to be surprised if the game came down to him getting a key hit or making a big play on defense. I told him if that was the situation, he had what it takes to deliver. I had no idea we would need him to win the game. The truth is, Cole making that play really didn't matter. What mattered to me was that he knew I had his back no matter what."

"Incredible," John said admiringly.

"Not really. It's all part of my *define why* when it comes to the team. My *why* is to love these boys, but as I said the other day, *love* is a verb. It's not enough for me to say I love them; I must show it in tangible ways. I have a chance to give life to them and build them up with my words."

"How exactly do your words tie into your why?"

"There's a proverb that says, 'Words kill, words give life; they're either poison or fruit—you choose.'* That basically means the guy who came up with the whole 'sticks and stones will break your bones' saying somehow had it wrong, and it's not just what we say but how we say it. The fact is, our words really can crush people, and they certainly can encourage. These kids have enough negative voices in their lives. I made up my mind I was going to be positive, no matter what. No matter how many errors, no matter how many mistakes, no matter how many times we lose a game. In fact, the scoreboard really isn't that important to me."

"It isn't?"

"It really isn't. What would it say about me if I let my success as a coach be defined by the light bulbs on a metal scoreboard at the Riverside Rec Center?"

"I don't know, maybe that you were a winning coach?"

Willie raised his voice. "Maybe not. If we won every game but had to tear kids down or cut corners, or failed to seize our opportunity to influence the next generation, I would consider myself a loser as a coach."

---

* Proverbs 18:21 MSG

14

Home Field Advantage

As Willie paused, John recalled his firm words and double standard with Ella about playing too rough. *"Words kill, words give life; they're either poison or fruit—you choose."* How many times had John chosen demanding words? Words that crushed confidence, doused dreams, or pointed out errors to his sweet daughters—words that killed? He himself was really the one at fault. His home, too often, had been one of lofty expectations and duty, not love. Emotion welled up as he considered the pain he had caused.

Willie's voice brought him back. "We're not babysitting here. And truthfully, we're not here to win games. We're here to build winners."

John refocused and nodded through the heaviness he was feeling as Willie continued, "When I first started coaching with Henry, he taught me a valuable lesson."

"What was that?" John asked.

"He told me one day that *'kids need to be validated more than they need to be tolerated'*—that most adults don't really see kids for who they are and what they can become. It changed my whole perspective and the way I coach."

"Kids need to be validated, not tolerated. Yeah, that sounds like Henry."

"This time, I'm going to take a guess. You're thinking about home. It's also true for kids at home. Spouses too. When we love people, we really see them and validate them for who they are. We recognize their errors are not rooted in bad intentions."

"Busted! I think I've been making way too many assumptions," John confessed.

"Think about it. Do you really believe your girls wake up in the morning and think, *I hope I mess up today so Dad will point it out to me*? Or that Kristen genuinely thinks, *I wonder if I can disappoint John?*"

"Probably not," John admitted.

"Definitely not. Part of loving first is giving your family members the benefit of the doubt. I like to ask myself what it's like to be on the other side of the table. You should try it the next time you're frustrated with someone at home."

"Have any suggestions?"

"Sure. Ask yourself, 'What's it like to be my daughter, and are my words giving life or sucking the life out of them?' Or, 'Does Kristen feel like I'm building up or diminishing her?' If you really desire to love first, you can start by giving the ones you love the home field advantage."

"The home field advantage, huh?"

"It works, John. I always remind myself that in a baseball game, the home team has the benefit of batting last, and they typically have more fans in the stands. You might say the game is tilted in their favor. At home, I want to tilt the game so Karen can feel like she is winning. I wanted the same for our sons before they left home."

"That makes sense. But what if I mess it up?"

"You will mess it up, every day. But if you really love first, Kristen and the girls will know and then you will know."

"How will I know? Know if it's working?"

"When the people who know you the best love you the most, it's working, my friend."

John's eyes brightened with hope. "If that's true, I'm guessing they might like me too," he said, thinking about his answer to Willie's *define why* and *decide what* blueprint exercise.

"It'll be a grand slam if the people who know you the best love you the most; but that will happen only if you take the initiative, if you love first. You're a winner, and winners go first. Unfortunately, I know too many people who love only if they feel loved. When that's the case, the people who know them the best respect them the least."

"Thanks for talking with me, Willie. I really appreciate your wisdom."

"It's my pleasure. Keep practicing and show up Tuesday night early. I think you're ready for part two of the strategy."

15

Bunting

Over the next couple of days, things began to slowly improve at home, but John knew something was still lacking. On Tuesday, he would begin to discover the missing piece.

Willie started Tuesday night's pre-practice huddle with the words, "Men, tonight will be the most important practice of our season."

With fourteen sets of young eyes glued on him, he continued, "Tonight we are going to learn what separates winners and losers. If you will truly lock in and master the concepts from this practice, you will always be a great teammate, and I can assure you, you're going to win both on and off the field. In fact, I've never known anyone to lose who embraced what I'm about to teach you."

As Willie paused, Timmy Turner spoke up. "Do you really think we can go undefeated, Coach?"

"Timmy, I believe you can win every game for the rest of your life if you understand and apply what you are about to learn."

Willie had their full attention. "Men, tonight we're going to learn how to bunt."

"Learn how to bunt?" three of the players said in unison.

"What does bunting have to do with winning?" Timmy asked.

"Bunting has everything to do with winning."

"I don't think they understand," John, also confused, piped in, hoping Willie would clarify.

"Most people don't understand. I think it's because almost everyone has a flawed understanding of winning. You see, boys, winning is so much more than who scores the most runs. The real winners are the ones who help other people win, the ones who refuse to fall into the trap of finding their identity based on the score of a game. Instead, they show up, and give up, so others can go up."

"That sounds like something Dr. Seuss would say," Cole Palmer said, causing his teammates and both coaches to laugh.

"Drew already knows how to bunt. He bunted in our very first game," Timmy reminded his coach.

Drew, who had played on Coach Carter's team last year and experienced this very practice, smiled at his coach with pride. "Just listen to Coach, guys. He knows what he's talking about."

BUNTING

"Thanks, Drew." Willie nodded to his star slugger. "Guys, when I was a kid playing Little League in this town like you, my dad was our coach. I was one of the oldest kids in the league. The year I turned twelve, aluminum bats had been invented, and I received one for Christmas. The first time I held it I remember thinking, *Life is about to become a whole lot easier. I'm about to hit dingers and dominate the league.* My dad, who loved baseball, had a different dream. He spent the entire spring teaching me how to bunt. While I had visions of home runs, he had visions of me sacrificing myself and moving runners over into scoring position by bunting. Let's just say we didn't see eye to eye at the time. But believe it or not, and I know it's hard for y'all to fathom, sometimes dads are right."

Most of the boys grinned as they thought about their struggles to listen to their own fathers.

"It was amazing," Willie continued to reflect. "We began to win, and I began to get a bunch of hits."

Timmy interrupted. "How did you get hits if you were bunting? I thought you said you were giving yourself up to move over your teammates so they could score."

"You may not believe this, but back in the day, I was pretty fast, and there wasn't a lot of bunting going on in the league. The other teams had a hard time adjusting. I bunted seventeen times during the season and advanced my teammates on the bases every single time. And because of my speed, I was thrown out only once.

As it happened, my willingness to sacrifice for others ultimately ended up being good for me too. We scored twice as many runs as we had the year before, and our team went undefeated, and Charles was named MVP of the league."

"Charles?" Timmy interrupted again.

"Yeah, my best friend, Charles, was in front of me in the lineup. Because of my bunting, he kept scoring runs, until he finally broke the league record. When he received his plaque, I must admit, I was a little jealous. He had a lot of help winning that award. I wasn't thinking the right way until my dad took me to Scoops. He let me order a double dip of strawberry and explained to me the most valuable player is the one who is willing to sacrifice the most for his teammates. He reminded me that while I ended up benefiting from giving myself up by getting on base, that sometimes real winners must be willing to lose so others can win . . . that even if I had been thrown out every single time, it would have ultimately made our team better. It's a lesson I never forgot and one we are going to learn tonight. Now let's get started."

Willie maximized every second of the next hour. He meticulously explained the fundamentals of bunting. He then paired the guys who had played on last year's team with the rookies and had them go first to demonstrate. Each pair had a single bat between them without a ball.

They took turns squaring up with soft, level hands, while their partner watched and gave feedback. The last forty-five minutes, Willie turned batting practice into bunting practice. No one was allowed to take a full swing. By the end, most of the kids at least looked like they knew what they were doing.

Willie closed the session by asking everyone to review the bunting fundamentals for at least five minutes each day until Saturday and to be ready to bunt if a situation came up where there was a runner on first or second with nobody out.

On Saturday, the Rangers indeed came ready. Riverside lit up the scoreboard like a pinball machine. Four times during the game, with runners on base, one of the boys laid down a perfect bunt and the merry-go-round started again on the bases. The 15–1 margin was mesmerizing as the Rangers scored in every inning.

When the game was over and the party ended, John asked Willie if he was headed home.

"Why, what did you have in mind?" Willie asked.

"I wanted to see if I could take you to Scoops for ice cream," John said with a smile. "After your brilliant coaching this week, I think a double dip of strawberry is warranted."

"Don't you have a house full of women waiting on you?"

"Actually, Kristen took her mom to a movie, and the girls are with their granddad for the afternoon."

"I'm in," Willie replied. "Karen is out of town this weekend for a women's conference, and I never turn down ice cream. I'll ride with you."

16

Scoops

The two coaches enjoyed postgame cheeseburgers and fries before moving on to the reason Riverside's most famous creamery was in business. The homemade ice cream recipes had drawn people from miles around for nearly sixty years. Willie had strawberry, and with the peaches in season, John couldn't resist.

"You said the other day you think I'm ready for the second part of the strategy. I'm wondering if this week's practice and today's game have anything to do with it?"

"Why do you say that?"

"Well, the whole sacrifice thing feels like it may have something to do with what is lacking in my marriage," John shared.

"Sounds like the dots are beginning to connect."

"They are, but I have a couple of questions."

"Let's hear them."

"First, why did you wait until this far into the season to have the bunting practice?"

"That's a good question. I always wait until we have a few games under our belts to teach bunting. The boys need to learn how to have fun first. Baseball is just a game, and bunting isn't as fun to a kid as swinging for the fences. What's your other question?"

"That makes sense. OK, remember the other night when you made the statement that the most valuable player is the one who is willing to sacrifice the most for his teammates? To use your words, if I connect the dots and see Kristen and my girls as my teammates, I'm not sure I have been putting them first. Truthfully, I think I have been putting myself first."

"John, it shows tremendous courage that you would be so vulnerable with me. I'm no expert, but what you're saying makes perfect sense. Most people don't want to live last."

"What do you mean by *live last*? I mean, I think I know, but explain in more detail."

"Sure. **Live last** is the second part of the strategy. Remember the other day when I said real winners show up, and give up, so others can go up?"

"I do. That's when Cole said you sounded like Dr. Seuss," John said with a chuckle.

"That's right. Well, it may sound like Dr. Seuss, but if you live last in all your relationships, it will also sound like music to the ears of the ones you love."

"Are you saying it has to be demonstrated through serving others?"

"Not exactly. Serving is an aspect, but real love moves to sacrifice," Willie said.

"Like bunting?"

"Bunting is a picture of it, just like a sacrifice fly or a bullpen full of relief pitchers."

"Sacrifice flies and relief pitchers? Sounds like the title of a bad baseball movie."

Willie laughed and continued, "My senior year of high school, we made it to the state championship game. I was on third base in the bottom of the last inning, and the score was tied with one out. Our batter hit a fly ball to the outfield, and when the ball was caught, I tagged up, sprinted for home to score the winning run, and received much of the glory. Our fans went nuts."

John said, "I remember my dad telling me about it when I got older. I was only three years old when it happened, but he was at the game."

"Everyone thought I was great because I scored and ended up being drafted by the Orioles. The truth is, Alan Davis is the one who was great that day."

"Alan Davis?"

"Alan Davis was the batter. He hit a home run in the fourth inning, and then when the game was on the line, he did for me what I did for Charles when I bunted all those times back in Little League. Alan made the out so I could score. In other words, he sacrificed so the team could win. Make no mistake, I was drafted because of my talent, but we won because of my teammate."

John's eyes brightened as if a light bulb had turned on.

Willie interrupted the revelation. "Here's the best part. Live last is perfectly designed to give you the results you want."

"I don't think I follow."

"Didn't you say you want a family that loves each other completely, no matter what? And one that likes each other as much as they love each other?"

"I did."

"Think about it, John. If you show a sacrificial mindset in your home and give up your rights to control, manipulate, or fix Kristen or any of the girls, how much more lovable do you think you'll be to each of them?"

"Probably a lot more."

"Certainly a lot more. I've never met a person who was turned off because they were too well loved."

"Yeah that makes sense."

"This is where the strategy is synced up. When a man or woman makes a decision to love first, it isn't enough."

"Why not?"

"The best leaders believe and behave their way to success. While *love* is a verb and drives behavior, it's also a feeling, or you might even say a belief. It doesn't reach its full potential until it is demonstrated. Until it is *behaved*. Living last is how you demonstrate that love is more than something you say, and that's where the bullpen comes in."

"I was wondering what the bullpen has to do with sacrifice flies."

"A bullpen full of relief pitchers is also a picture of living last."

"You lost me on that one, Willie."

"You know how the bullpen is full of pitchers who literally enter the game last, often expected to clean up a big mess made by a tired starting pitcher or a fielder who makes a bad error? They are one of the ultimate groups of people who live last. They rarely get the credit, but regardless, the bullpen is typically expected to save the day and preserve victory."

"I assume you're suggesting I should be the bullpen at home?"

Grinning, Willie nodded. "How often do you suppose Kristen is exhausted when you walk in the door at the end of the day?"

"Pretty often." John stated the obvious as he considered the challenge of a full day with the twins, not to mention the baby.

"What if you truly started showing up as a relief parent and gave the tired starting parent a break? Don't you think it would communicate to Kristen how important she is and that you are committed to helping her win?"

Willie's questions ushered in a wave of sadness for John, recognizing his effort to give Kristen a break a few days ago wasn't nearly enough. He thought of how relief pitchers were available game after game and realized he needed to show up every day for his wife.

"How often do your girls fail to act like adults?"

"Should they act like adults?" John answered a bit defensively.

"No. They should act like kids. Maybe I should ask it another way. How many times do you expect them to act like adults and find yourself frustrated because they are acting like kids?"

"Guilty as charged," John acknowledged.

"John, I'm not charging you, and I don't want you to feel guilty. I'm just telling you from experience that it's easy to have lofty expectations for those we love and give ourselves a pass, when we may be the real problem."

"It's something I need to work on."

"I know. It's hard to live last—to bunt, so to speak, so others can score. When my dad was teaching me to bunt as a kid, in his wisdom, he was really teaching me what it would be like to be an adult. As a dad, I found myself bunting for my kids all the time, providing them with opportunities to score through tuition payments, transportation, attendance at their activities, and investing in them at home with my time. As a husband, I've learned that if I want to win, I need to help Karen win first. Any time I seize an opportunity to help make her life easier, it actually benefits us both. Dad was right: real winners sacrifice so others can win."

"You've given me more to think about."

Willie ended the conversation with, "Let me encourage you to keep fighting for your family, and don't be surprised if you find yourself tested."

17

Strike Two

The test would come within the hour. John, reeling from the conversation with Willie, was pulling in the driveway when he was caught off guard by the flashing lights of an ambulance next door. His heart sank as he assumed Coach Henry had suffered a heart attack. As he ran across the property line, he was surprised to see Carol, strapped to a gurney, being wheeled out the front door. Henry rushed out onto the porch, full of emotion, following his wife of forty-three years.

"What can I do for you, Coach?" John asked as Henry spotted him.

"She fell and . . . and I need to get to the hospital."

"Hop in, I'll drive you, and we can follow the ambulance."

For the next three hours, John sat with Henry at Riverside Regional as Carol had emergency surgery for a fractured hip. The waiting room was right outside the ER where he had first met Kristen.

Henry now resembled the loved ones in the ICU waiting room John had observed with Willie—albeit without his loved one with him. Still, the affection overflowed, and Henry appeared to be in even more pain than his wife had been in as she was rolled into the ambulance.

"She's been through so much," Henry remarked, his voice quavering, still overwhelmed with emotion. "With my heart troubles, and now . . . now this. But she's strong. The strongest person I know. She's my hero."

To hear Henry talk about his wife in such endearing terms caused John to feel envy. He had once felt and said similar things about Kristen. As the doctor appeared and spoke privately with Henry, John realized how much he wanted to have a stronger family bond and suddenly felt motivated to put in the work.

Henry came back to tell him the good news that all was well so far and that he'd likely be spending the night. John offered to come back to pick him up or bring a car the next morning. Henry said, "I'll let you know."

As John walked to the elevator, he checked his phone and realized he'd left it on silent, and, distracted by Henry, he'd lost track of time and forgotten to check in with Kristen. He had missed eleven calls and four texts from her. He dialed home and she frantically answered on the first ring.

"Where are you!" she shouted bitingly.

Love first and live last were the furthest things from John's mind as he raised his voice back. "I'm at the hospital with Henry!"

"Oh no, is he OK?" Kristen quickly softened.

John, still feeling attacked, followed with, "It's not him; it's Carol. She fell and broke her hip and had to have emergency surgery. I drove Henry and forgot to call you. I'm sorry."

"We were worried sick about you. When will you be home?"

"I'm headed that way," John abruptly answered before clicking off the call. This was a fastball moment, and John had swung and missed again.

As he drove home, John thought of Willie. He could almost hear his voice. *"Live last."* Kristen was genuinely concerned and had every right to wonder where he was. He thought, *How could I be so stupid?*

By the time he reached the house, the words *live last* had reframed his mind and heart. When he walked in, Kristen met him at the back door with a forgiving hug and a soft kiss under his left eye.

"Thank God you're OK! I'm sorry for overreacting," she said. He was about to apologize in return but thought it might seem insincere, as if he was just saying sorry because she said it first.

Instead, he leaned in to feeling loved, missed, and in some odd way, wanted. Blindsided with his own emotions, this was the moment John knew that if he put in the effort, they would have the kind of family he hoped for.

18

Contract Extension

On Tuesday, John swung by the hospital to check on Carol before practice. She was recovering nicely, but it was going to be a couple more days before she was released and then another month of rehab. As he was leaving her room, Henry walked him out into the hallway and asked if he might be willing to consider completing the season as assistant coach. The request gave John an idea.

When he pulled into the fields for practice, he found Willie sitting in his truck finishing up a phone call.

"I heard you're making the hospital your home away from home," Willie said.

"Where did you hear that?"

"I was just on the phone with an old bird. I also hear you might be looking for a contract extension. I thought that might be the case, seeing as how this is your last week on the job. I'm willing to consider keeping you, but don't be asking for more money," Willie said with a grin.

"Actually, I do want to discuss my contract." John returned the smile.

"Oh?" Willie questioned.

"I did talk to Henry, and sadly he informed me he might be out for the year. He wondered if I might be willing to go the distance with you. I told him I would, but before we ink the deal I was wondering if you might do me a favor."

"I might. What did you have in mind?"

"I need some coaching. As you have probably figured out by now, things have been strained for Kristen and me. I thought you might be able to share some secrets to a meaningful marriage."

Willie smiled as he answered, "John, I'm not a counselor."

"I know; all the better. I'm not looking for therapy. Well, maybe I am, but let's start with a little coaching. You've already given me so much to think about, and I really do want to win at home. If you're willing to help me there, I'm willing to help you here."

Willie stuck out his big hand and the deal was sealed. He then reached into the bed of his truck and grabbed the rakes, handing one to John. As they made their way to the field, John filled Willie in on the weekend's events surrounding Carol and Henry, and also his failure to communicate with Kristen that he was at the hospital.

He also told him about how he was short with her after the phone call and how she apologized when he walked in the door.

As the two began dragging the infield, Willie asked, "Did you apologize to her?"

"Not exactly. I wanted to, but I didn't want to come across as apologizing just because she apologized."

"You like to make things harder than they have to be, don't you?" Willie asked.

"I guess I do. I really do want to live last, but I have no idea how to consistently do it. I'm not sure why, but I'm still struggling."

"There are a couple of secrets to living last if you're interested in hearing about them."

"Absolutely. Do you think they'll really help?"

"I know they will. At least they did for me."

"Let me hear them."

"The first secret is to *stop making a big deal out of small things*."

"Can you give me an example?"

"Sure. It's what you did Saturday night when Kristen asked you where you were. I know it's none of my business, but it makes sense to me that she would have been concerned. I'll give you that maybe she didn't ask in the right way, but what if you had decided to give her a pass on that and seen her concern as a positive?"

"I actually thought about that on the ride home after I snapped at her."

"John, I spent the first few years of my marriage making a big deal out of small things. Karen could never do anything right—at least that's what I communicated to her. The truth is, I'm the one who messed up the most."

"Don't make a big deal out of small things. That makes sense. So what's the second secret?"

"This one is very important. *Don't make the mistake of reversing the order of the strategy.* I had the order reversed for a while." Willie paused and stood upright with both hands folded on top of his rake. As John looked up, Willie continued, "Instead of love first and live last, I was living first and loving last."

John stood as well, leaned on his own rake, and nodded as if he understood.

"The strategy works only if you get the order right. Unfortunately, I was putting myself first and loving Karen last. That's a recipe for disaster. Remember how I said when you love first you give the other person the benefit of the doubt? I realized I was doing the opposite. I was loving myself first and doubting Karen."

"Ouch. I think I can relate," John admitted.

"It wasn't good. I thought about my needs, my rights, my desires, and my dreams. In the meantime, I was trampling hers."

"I feel like this is one of those 'easier said than done' things. How did you learn to live last consistently?"

"Pay attention at practice and I think it will become clear."

19

Slumps

Willie began practice by saying, "Young men, did I ever tell you about the time I had a twenty-one game hitting streak when I was playing in the minors?"

John, never knowing Willie to be anything but humble, was surprised by the opening statement. Most of the boys' dads had told them Willie had played in the minors, so they sat wide-eyed with anticipation.

"Those four weeks turned out to be the best I ever hit the ball, but to be honest, right before the streak, I was in an awful slump. I actually went thirty-seven consecutive plate appearances without a hit. It became so bad I struck out nine times in a row. It was as if I had forgotten how to hit a baseball. I was ready to quit the game and head back to Riverside. Fortunately for me, our hitting coach asked me to join him for lunch on the day my streak started. I thought he might tell me to pack my bags because I was being let go from the team.

"There was no one I respected as much as him. The man knew more about hitting than anyone I had ever met. He was constantly pounding us with the fundamentals of vision, rhythm, timing, and balance. As we sat and chatted over fish tacos, he told me a story about the best hitter he ever coached. It turns out the guy was in a tremendous slump just like the one I was in. Coach said he had a secret whenever someone was in a deep slump. I asked him what it was, and he said he wanted me to forget the fundamentals. *'Don't even think about them tonight,'* he told me. I asked him what he wanted me to think about, and he said, *'Let's simplify it to two things. See ball; hit ball.'"*

The boys laughed at the simplicity of *see ball; hit ball.*

"Guys, I don't know what happened, but it was as if my mind was freed up. I had four hits that night with two doubles and a triple. The next three weeks the baseball looked like a beach ball. I kept seeing it and hitting it. It's actually how I got called up to Double A, which is as far as I ever made it."

"But we're not in a slump. We scored fifteen runs on Saturday; that's not slumpy," Drew said, causing everyone to laugh, including Willie.

"True. I'm telling you this because I wanted to remind you that baseball is supposed to be fun. It's just a game, and sometimes it's easy for us to make a bigger deal out of it than it is." He looked over at John as he said this, causing *"Don't make a big deal out of small things"* to flash through John's mind.

"There will come a time when you will find yourself struggling to do what you know how to do. When that time comes, return to the basics. Just see it, hit it, and have fun."

The next hour was mesmerizing as the boys pounded line drive after line drive.

There was laughter in the air as joy filled the sandlot. John was taken back to his childhood as he remembered how much fun he had playing on Henry's first team.

After practice, he couldn't wait to ask Willie about his story. As was their habit, the two walked out to the parking lot together.

"Why did you share about your slump tonight?"

"To be honest, I thought you needed to hear it. It appears to me you are in a live-last slump. That's what you said before practice. That you know what to do but find yourself struggling to do it."

"OK, but that's not like a game, so what does that have to do with *your* slump?"

"The place to start with living last is the place I needed to start with my hitting. But instead of 'see ball, hit ball,' you need to 'see need, meet need.'"

"A little simple, don't you think?" John asked, connecting the dots.

"Perhaps you're making it too hard. What if you forgot about a list of marital obligations and just started looking for a need to meet. Anytime one showed up, no matter how large or small, you leveraged your time, energy, and effort to meet the need. What effect do you think it would have?"

"It can't be that easy," John responded.

"Have you tried it?"

"I can't say I have."

"Well, maybe you should before you knock it," Willie challenged him.

"See need, meet need," John said aloud as Willie opened the truck door.

As he cranked up the engine, he rolled down the window, looked John in the eyes, and said, "Congratulations."

"For what?"

"Your new contract," Willie said with a wink. "I knew you had more than four weeks in you."

20

A Setback

Wednesday through Friday were days of ups and downs at home. John found himself recognizing opportunities to help more than usual. Each time, he responded quickly, meeting needs without expecting anything in return, but he had a setback on Thursday.

After dinner, Kristen headed to the gym, leaving John and the twins to clear the dishes. He was in a hurry to move the girls toward bedtime so he could have some time to work on a project he had been putting off for a week. Hannah Kate, wanting to help, climbed up a barstool and onto the kitchen counter, then accidentally pushed the fishbowl off the edge, causing it to crack, water to splash all over the floor, and the betta fish the twins had named Raymond to flop for dear life. John went into hero mode and saved the fish by placing it in Hannah Kate's sippy cup, which thankfully was half full of water. With wide eyes, Hannah Kate clapped with delight and squealed, "Daddy!" as she sat on the counter beside the sink. No harm done until Ella yelled at Hannah Kate. This caused John to yell at Ella and send her to her room as he inspected the cracked fishbowl. Emma, who notoriously avoided conflict, suddenly welled up with tears, and John, not wanting to deal with the crying, sent her upstairs to join Ella. Predictably, his tone caused Hannah Kate to cry too.

A minute later, a refreshed Kristen walked in the door and asked where the twins were. John answered tersely, "Don't ask!" ensuring a perfect four for four on alienating the people who mattered most to him. He handed her the crying baby, grabbed his keys, and stormed out the door, leaving Kristen to clean up the mess—literal and emotional.

John, disgusted with himself, dashed off to the pet store before closing time to find a new fishbowl. He made the purchase and headed back toward home, intending to make things right with the girls before bedtime. As he started the car, the engine failed to turn over. A dead battery. *You have to be kidding me*, he thought as he lowered his head onto the top of the steering wheel. *This cannot be happening.*

Assessing his options, he considered calling Kristen, but she would be bathing the baby and preparing the twins for bed and might not even take his call. Besides, there was no way he could expect her to load the girls into the van and come to his rescue. He decided the best bet this late was to walk the mile and a half back and worry about the car in the morning. John set out on a thirty-minute hike home carrying a fishbowl.

21

The Power of a Walk

Saturday's game with Riverside's other team, the Cubs, came down to the wire. The Rangers' pitchers struggled all day, but the bats kept them in it until the last inning. Both teams easily surpassed Willie's rule of seven, entering the last inning knotted 11 to 11.

The Cubs loaded the bases with one out but failed to score when Cole Palmer snagged a line drive and doubled up a runner who had streaked off second on the crack of the bat.

Timmy Turner led off the bottom of the inning with a single. The next two Rangers made outs, and then suddenly the Cubs' fourth pitcher of the day, a wiry kid named Morgan, couldn't find the strike zone. He walked the next two hitters and loaded the bases. With no one else available to pitch, the Cubs manager left Morgan in to face Drew Duncan. Morgan's next four pitches were nowhere close. When the umpire yelled ball four, Timmy strolled home and the Rangers again found themselves victorious.

Both teams congratulated each other after it was over, recognizing they had played in one of the wildest games of the year.

"That was close," John said as he slapped Willie on the back.

"That's an understatement. Isn't it amazing how powerful a walk can be?"

Why do I have the feeling there's more behind that statement than what just happened? John wondered.

Suddenly, one of the moms offered to buy each of the boys a hot dog for winning. The entire team let out an exuberant yell and sprinted to the concession stand, leaving John and Willie in the dugout to pack up the equipment.

"What did you mean by a walk can be powerful?" John asked Willie as he held open the bat bag.

"Why do you ask?"

John proceeded to tell Willie about Thursday night's setback and how he ended up walking home from the pet store. The admission caused Willie to laugh.

"Seriously, Willie, I felt like a fool toting a fishbowl down Riverside Drive, but in a crazy way the walk felt like a powerful moment. It really gave me time to think and do some soul-searching."

"And?"

"And, I keep failing. I keep wanting things to be right, but I'm the one who keeps getting them wrong."

"That's part of what I meant when I said a walk can be powerful," Willie stated, now more serious. "I saw you walking down Riverside Thursday night and started to stop. But I had a feeling you probably could use the space, so I left you to your 'soul-searching.'"

"Thanks for not stopping," John remarked sarcastically.

"You're welcome. *Taking time to think before you act often determines whether you live last or live first.* The dead battery slowed you down and made you walk, giving you time to reflect."

As John thought back on the walk home, he knew Willie was right. He had cooled off before he made it home and, accordingly, had apologized to everyone when he arrived.

Willie interrupted John's thoughts. "But that's only the first part."

"What's the second part?"

"*Love goes slow.* Until I learned that, I was always leaving everyone behind."

"Love goes slow. I've never heard it phrased like that."

"Think about it. Most leaders, like yourself, feel a sense of urgency to chase their vision and conquer the mountain. If they're not careful, it's easy to run off and leave their people. But remember, *winning begins at home.* It's easy for a mom or dad to run ahead of their kids or for a spouse to leave their partner behind. The truth is, you can't be running if everyone else is walking, or you will leave them in the dust. Speed kills intimacy, my friend."

"Ouch," John said as he considered how often he had tried to hurry Kristen and the girls.

"Sounds like I struck a nerve," Willie said with a grin.

"Guilty again, which raises another question."

"Fire away."

"Remember how you told me a couple of weeks ago I would know I'm loving first when the people who know me the best love me the most?"

Willie nodded. "I sure do."

"Well, how will I know if I'm living last?"

"That's easy. When you make the decision to live last, in effect you're deciding to move to the back of the line. When everyone in your family is in front of you, you'll know you have it right."

John cinched up the bat bag and threw it over his shoulder. Before he could respond, his cell vibrated. The screen showed a call from Kristen.

22

Winning at Home

John drove slowly across town, allowing Willie's wisdom to sink in and processing what he wanted to say. Kristen had called to let him know the girls were staying with her parents for the night, and she wanted to know if he would like to go out for dinner.

Instead, he had asked if he could grab takeout so they could eat at home. She agreed and requested Chinese.

He pulled in the garage, killed the engine, and reached for the sack full of warm boxes. He walked into the kitchen and set the food beside the new fishbowl just as Kristen walked in from the back and said, "That smells great."

This time it was John who led with, "We need help . . . We can't go on like this."

Before she could say a word, he took her by the hand and led her to the island and pulled out two barstools. "I need to apologize for Thursday night. Actually, I need to apologize for a lot more than Thursday."

John's words were so unexpected, tears immediately began streaming down Kristen's face.

For the next hour, while the food became cold, John was honest with his wife as she had been with him months ago. He acknowledged his mistakes and expressed his desire for a better marriage. He opened up about how he had used work as an escape and found his validation at the office rather than home. And for the first time, he told her about the blueprint he had been working on, explaining what kind of family he wanted them to have. He asked her to forgive him for his selfishness and vowed to continue making changes.

Kristen listened attentively, astounded with her husband's vulnerability and fresh perspective. They both wept and laughed at different points of his transparency.

John caressed her hand and looked deeply into Kristen's eyes. "I know it's easy for me to prioritize work, but I've become convinced that winning begins at home, and I think I've been losing here most of the time. Kristen, if I win at work and lose at home, I would consider that losing. I love you with all my heart, and I want to win here first."

After a long pause, Kristen finally spoke. "So where do we go from here?"

Without hesitation, John responded, "I think we need a coach. Actually, I already have one."

"A coach?"

"A coach. Do you know how some couples go to marriage counseling?"

"Truthfully, I've wondered if it's something we should consider."

"I've wondered the same thing, but I'm not sure I'm ready to try anything that clinical. What if we could find someone a little less formal who could help us?"

"Like who?"

"Like Willie."

"Willie? I thought he was a baseball coach. What does he know about coaching families?"

"Actually, quite a lot. He's been coaching me, and I know I have a long way to go, but I've learned so much from him the last few weeks. I thought it might be a good idea for us to ask him and his wife, Karen, if we can take them out to dinner."

"I don't know, John. That feels kind of strange. What would we say?"

"I'm not sure we would have to say anything. What if we just listened? Everything the guy says is so wise. I believe it would be good for us to hear from an older couple who has navigated some of the stormy waters we are in. Besides, Willie told me there was a time when things were hard for them too. I'm beginning to understand, more and more, that marriage isn't easy. Maybe we could ask them their secrets?" John concluded with a hopeful smile.

"If that's what you want, I'm in. I can tell you are different, and if you think Willie and his wife can help, who am I to argue?"

"I'll talk to him."

"Thank you," she affirmed.

"It's no big deal. I'm sure he'll be willing."

"No, thank you for tonight. I had almost given up on the idea of things ever being better. Maybe together, we really can do this. Now, let's eat."

23

Late to Practice

John pulled up to the field right as practice was ending. "We missed you, Coach," several of the players said in passing as they filled the parking lot looking for the correct SUV or minivan.

John waved to the boys before walking to the outfield fence, opening the latch, and striding across the grass to catch up to Willie, who was headed toward the dugout to collect the equipment.

"Look who showed up. I wasn't expecting to see you tonight," Willie boomed with joy. John had called on Sunday and told him he might have to miss because of an out-of-town consulting gig but would do everything he could to make it.

"I apologize again, Coach. Summer storms caused airports to bog down in the Midwest, and I couldn't get an earlier flight home," John said as they each picked up a bag.

"Not a problem, but don't be surprised if I have to fine you."

"I'm good with that. You can deduct it from my pay," John bantered back.

"We missed you."

"Thanks, how did it go tonight?"

"It went great. The boys are really beginning to understand how to win."

"I think they already have winning down. We haven't lost yet."

"I might have to challenge you on that."

"But we're undefeated."

"I'll give you we have scored more runs than our opponents in every game, but I wouldn't say we are undefeated. It all depends on how you keep score."

"Willie, I usually have a hard time following you at first, but this time you have totally lost me."

"Winning is not about how many runs we score or how few we give up. I thought we covered that a few weeks ago. Winning is about dominating what you can control."

"Dominating what you can control, huh?"

"Yes, sir. I learned that from a leadership speaker who came and spoke to our team during spring training my first year in the minors."

"This ought to be good," John chuckled.

"Hear me out. This guy was a really good speaker who typically worked with businesses. Our GM had heard about him and invited him to come and speak to our entire organization. There were several hundred scouts, coaches, office staff, and both major and minor league players. One of our team values was to control the controllables. The leadership guy stands up and the first thing he says is he thought we should do away with our value of controlling the controllables. It really let the air out of the room. I thought the GM might throw him out of camp on the spot. That is, until his next statement.

"He said, 'If something is controllable, a real winner doesn't worry about controlling it. Champions dominate the controllables.' I don't remember anything else he said, but it rocked my world to hear him challenge us to dominate what we could control. It's what I've been trying to do ever since."

"That's powerful. Can you give me an example of how it changed your approach?"

"You bet. Think about an athlete. They have total control over their preparation, their desire, their attitude, and their work ethic. There is no reason those things shouldn't be dominated. The same is true for a husband and father. Obviously, you can't control how Kristen or the girls feel or act toward you, but you can control how you think and act toward them. When you decide to love first and live last, it gets fleshed out when you dominate your attitude, approach them with positivity, lower your expectations, and speak words of affirmation. Those are all choices. They are your opportunity to run up the score at home."

Run up the score? John pondered.

"Consider all you've been through the last few months. You said yourself home has been a real challenge. I certainly can relate. Home is the hardest place you will ever lead. It's why winning must begin there. The reality is, when you win at home, the rest of life becomes so much easier. As you have discovered, you will always find yourself falling short of perfect. John, there are no perfect families."

"Ours certainly isn't."

"Ours either. If you're like me, you will often feel like you're losing the game because of things beyond your control. That's why I always try to dominate the things I can control. I figure the more times I can help my family score, the more those runs will come in handy later. It's almost like a bank account. When you dominate the things you can control, it's like making deposits with compound interest. Later, when things get hard—and they will—you will have a surplus of love to draw from."

"That's awesome, Willie."

"Now, go home and start running up the score. After being out of town for a couple of days, you have no business being here."

"Before I go, I want to ask you for another favor. Would you and Karen allow Kristen and me to buy you dinner?"

Not surprisingly, Willie agreed dinner with the wives was a great idea. But rather than going out, he asked John if Kristen would be open to the idea of coming to their home for dinner. John tried to convince him to let them treat, but Willie stood firm.

When John relented, they agreed the following Friday would work great.

24
Dinner

John and Kristen held hands as they approached Willie's humble ranch-style home. John pushed the doorbell and took a deep breath. They were both surprised when a lovely woman in her midfifties opened the door seated in a wheelchair and said, "Welcome to our home. I'm Karen Carter."

She called over her shoulder, "Willie, our guests are here."

Willie walked into the foyer with a big, broad smile on his face and said, "Dear, this is John, and you must be Kristen. John is my assistant this year with the boys. He's the one I told you about, who thought he could take Henry's place."

Karen, with a smile on her face, said, "No one could possibly take Henry's place." The four of them shared a laugh as John heartily agreed.

"Follow me, folks. I hope everyone likes Italian." Karen turned the wheelchair toward the heart of the home.

"It's my favorite," John said with anticipation as they entered the kitchen.

The rest of the evening was delightful. Willie had John tell the ladies about the season and all they had experienced together. With appreciation, John explained how he had reluctantly agreed to take Henry's place—causing another chuckle from the group—and how the season had not really been about baseball for him. It had actually been a crash course in how to save a family.

"Willie, I will forever be in debt to you. I know I'm just getting started, but I'm committed to doing the necessary work to be a better husband and father, and I wouldn't have gotten here without you."

"It's a never-ending journey, my friend. This is just the beginning. I'm confident you will keep making progress," Willie said, winking at John.

Karen beamed with pride as she looked at her man. Noticing her gaze toward Willie, John couldn't help but think, *That's what it looks like when the person who knows you the best loves you the most.*

"Thank you, Willie!" John exclaimed.

"For what?"

"For teaching me that *winning begins at home*."

PART TWO

WINNING BEGINS AT HOME

ACTIVATION GUIDE

ACTIVATION GUIDE

You might not consider your marriage, family, or homelife as a "competition" in the same way baseball games or sales targets are. But you *are* competing—every single day—and the competition is against your former self. Are you a better spouse than you were yesterday? Are you a more loving parent than you were last year? Are you a better sibling, friend, son, or daughter than you were in the past? As you muster the courage to answer these questions, you need to put a strategy in place. One of the first lessons Willie taught John was, "A strategy is needed any time you compete."

The following Activation Guide should serve as a framework for this strategy, guiding you to create a blueprint, like John, to build the life you want.

A few important things to note:

- ◆ Transformation won't happen overnight. In fact, the *end* of this story was just the *beginning* of John's journey to winning at home. The process to loving first and living last will take daily dedication, persistent patience, and a commitment to progress over perfection.
- ◆ You must start where you are. Be honest as you work through the guide and vulnerable as you confront the cracks in the foundation of your homelife. Remember, while you must start where you are, you don't have to stay there.

- Anybody can do it! Winning at work and at home isn't impossible. There is no secret key or superhero skill needed. It simply requires a commitment to the strategy you are about to create so you can confidently say the people who know you the best love you the most.

Let's get started!

Winning Begins at Home Assessment

For the following questions, think carefully and circle the answer that best describes your current behavior.

1. **I demonstrate my love for those closest to me rather than only saying it.**

   Never   Rarely   Sometimes   Frequently   Always

2. **I control my words, tone, and volume even when I am angry, stressed, or upset.**

   Never   Rarely   Sometimes   Frequently   Always

3. **When disputes arise, I give my loved ones the benefit of the doubt.**

   Never   Rarely   Sometimes   Frequently   Always

4. **I sacrifice my own desires if it means a loved one will benefit.**

   Never   Rarely   Sometimes   Frequently   Always

5. I serve others without expecting anything in return.
   Never   Rarely   Sometimes   Frequently   Always

6. I add, rather than extract, value at home.
   Never   Rarely   Sometimes   Frequently   Always

7. I lead by setting a positive, integrity-based example for my household.
   Never   Rarely   Sometimes   Frequently   Always

8. I strive to improve who I am as a leader at home and assess myself frequently.
   Never   Rarely   Sometimes   Frequently   Always

9. I devote time to working toward the vision of the life I am trying to build.
   Never   Rarely   Sometimes   Frequently   Always

10. I work hard not to overreact and make a big deal out of small things.
    Never   Rarely   Sometimes   Frequently   Always

11. I know what I can control in my home life and work toward dominating these areas.
    Never   Rarely   Sometimes   Frequently   Always

12. After work, my family gets the best of me rather than the rest of me.
    Never   Rarely   Sometimes   Frequently   Always

13. **My calendar reflects that I prioritize the people I love the most.**

    Never   Rarely   Sometimes   Frequently   Always

14. **My behaviors align with my values when it comes to how I treat my loved ones.**

    Never   Rarely   Sometimes   Frequently   Always

15. **When I see a need at home, I meet that need.**

    Never   Rarely   Sometimes   Frequently   Always

Note any items where you circled *Sometimes*, *Rarely*, or *Never*. Remember, the purpose of this assessment is to bring awareness to where you need to improve before you move into developing your blueprint.

The Prerequisites

Now it's time to create the blueprint for the life you want, which begins with laying the groundwork. As John did, you must **Define What** and **Decide Why**.

In the story, Willie said, "If you can define what kind of family you want and decide why you want to have a family, you will be perfectly positioned to win at home." The goal is to win consistently. With your blueprint in place, your efforts toward the vision will be **strategic instead of sporadic!**

DEFINE WHAT

Think about *what* the vision of your family looks like. These could be abstract *what*s (like John's concept of a family with unconditional love and one that "likes each other as much as we love each other") or more tangible *what*s (such as a family who sits down for dinner together every night, or one with members who show up to support one another's events).

What does the family you want look like? Take time to picture it; put yourself there.

On the next page, label the blueprint with your family name and then write down what you see.

Remember, you can come back to this blueprint, edit it, add on to it, and so forth. Don't feel pressured to envision your ideal family in one sitting!

Family Blueprint

Last Name:

_____
_____
_____
_____
_____
_____
_____
_____
_____
_____
_____
_____
_____
_____

What are three things you can do this week to move toward the life you have envisioned?

_____

_____

_____

What are three things you can do this month to move toward the life you have envisioned?

_____

_____

_____

What are three things you can do this year to move toward the life you have envisioned?

_____

_____

_____

DECIDE WHY

What is your motivation to build the family you described on the preceding pages? If you don't have a driving force, a change in your actions is unlikely. John desired joy, fun, and serving others, but only you can come up with your own personal motivations. So what is your family *why*?

_____

_____

_____

_____

_____

_____

_____

_____

_____

_____

_____

_____

_____

_____

_____

_____

Great! You have **Defined What** and **Decided Why** (or at least started the ball rolling).

As you build on your blueprint and undertake the actions you listed on page 136 in the next week, month, and year, it's also critical to find your mentor. Who will you learn from? Who will hold you responsible for sticking to your strategic plan? These roles may be fulfilled by the same person, or you may find various people to serve as a coach, mentor, counselor, and/or accountability partner.

Think of a few now.

Who are a few people who serve in the same role as you in life (for example, an executive and a mother, or another teacher who is also the father of toddlers) but you think do it *better* than you? List them here and what you hope to learn from them:

Mentor: _____
What I hope to learn:

_____

_____

_____

Mentor: _____
What I hope to learn:

_____

_____

_____

Mentor: _____

What I hope to learn:

_____

_____

_____

Now, who will you ask to hold you accountable on your path of self-improvement?

_____

_____

_____

What does this realistically look like (e.g., weekly phone calls, regular self-assessments, monthly meetings, etc.)?

_____

_____

_____

The Fundamentals

Now, with the prerequisites established, it's time to tackle the fundamentals. We'll start with the big ideas—**Love First** and **Live Last**—and discuss a few key Things to Remember under each. Within each of the Things to Remember, you will be tasked with an exercise to complete as well as some recommended next steps. Some of the exercises will require you to relive past, perhaps painful, experiences, and some will also involve your loved ones' participation.

FUNDAMENTALS STEP 1

Love First

As Willie said, "*Love* is the most powerful word in the history of the world . . . *Love* is not just a noun. *Love* is also a verb."

We'll dive deeper into "*Love* is a verb" under the first Things to Remember, but first, let's define **love**.

Willie said, "It is considerate, kind, resilient, patient, and thoughtful."

How do you define what love is (**noun**)?
_____
_____
_____

How do you define what love does (**verb**)?
_____
_____
_____

What **adjectives** would you use to define *love*, beyond what Willie listed?
_____
_____
_____

Love First

Things to Remember #1: *Love* Is a Verb

It is not enough to simply tell our loved ones we love them—although we should be doing that too! We must also demonstrate it. **Love is a verb** and can be demonstrated in countless ways—such as doing household chores no one wants to do, helping with homework, being a better listener, or allotting quality time for the people who matter most. Are you treating *love* as a verb? Do the exercise below to find out.

Exercise

How are you currently demonstrating love at home? Think through this question and then write down a few recent or recurring examples:

_____
_____
_____
_____
_____
_____
_____
_____

Now, ask your loved ones to answer the same question. How do they see you demonstrating love? List their answers here:

_____

_____

_____

_____

_____

_____

Finally, ask your loved ones one more question: How *could* you demonstrate love toward them? This could include tasks or actions you haven't ever considered or may simply be performing the aforementioned activities more frequently. Give them a day or two to think on this, if needed. Record their answers here and bookmark this page for future reference!

_____

_____

_____

_____

_____

_____

Next Steps

In addition to your loved ones' list, draft your own creative ideas for how you can show love in the following lines. This may require some deep digging, outside research, or conversations with friends or the mentors you identified on pages 138–139.

_____

_____

_____

_____

_____

_____

_____

_____

_____

Once you have both lists, choose two to three items to tackle immediately. Next week, add on another. Continue this until you are demonstrating love in every way you know how.

Love First

Things to Remember #2: Love Is a Choice

Although you are working toward the idealized vision of the life you want to build, you must also remember there are no perfect marriages, nor are there perfect people. We are all inherently flawed. Life would be boring if we weren't!

However, you must also remember that **love is a choice**. Choosing love means choosing to see the good over the flaws. It means giving your loved ones the benefit of the doubt. And it means choosing to validate—not just tolerate—people.

Are you actively choosing love? Engage with the exercise below to see.

Exercise

There's only one rule for this exercise. Complete the following task without peeking at the follow-up instructions on page 151.

On the following lines, choose up to four loved ones and list out **ten** adjectives to describe each person. This list is for your eyes only, so feel free to say whatever is on your heart.

THE FUNDAMENTALS

Name: _____

Adjectives:

1. _____
2. _____
3. _____
4. _____
5. _____
6. _____
7. _____
8. _____
9. _____
10. _____

WINNING BEGINS AT HOME

Name: _____

Adjectives:

1. _____
2. _____
3. _____
4. _____
5. _____
6. _____
7. _____
8. _____
9. _____
10. _____

THE FUNDAMENTALS

Name: _____

Adjectives:

1. _____
2. _____
3. _____
4. _____
5. _____
6. _____
7. _____
8. _____
9. _____
10. _____

WINNING BEGINS AT HOME

Name: _____

Adjectives:

1. _____
2. _____
3. _____
4. _____
5. _____
6. _____
7. _____
8. _____
9. _____
10. _____

Great. Hopefully you didn't look ahead and you have your lists completed.

Now, look at the ten adjectives you've chosen for each person. How many of these adjectives have a positive connotation? How many have a negative connotation? Are you seeking the good in each person, or are you more inclined to notice their flaws?

Think of how each person would describe you if they had to choose ten adjectives. Wouldn't you rather they notice the good?

Next Steps

Choosing love and always seeing the good can require a brain shift. Here are some daily actions you can do to actually rewire the way you think!

- **Start every morning with a compliment.** Don't make it formulaic or forced, but simply start each day with an intention of seeing the good. Can the first words out of your mouth each morning be a compliment? Try it out and see how that one simple action changes your entire day.
- **Assume positive intent.** In each and every interaction—especially when it comes to disagreements!—assume the other person is being honest and trying their best. Don't scoff

at others' excuses or apologies; instead, believe them and forgive them. Try this technique moving forward (it may be unnatural at first!) and see how it transforms your relationships.

- **End every night with gratitude.** Keep a gratitude journal by your bedside. Each night, write three to five things you are grateful for. Studies show that cultivating an attitude of gratitude reduces levels of the stress hormone cortisol in the body by 23 percent.[5]

Love First

Things to Remember #3: You're Never Persuasive When You're Abrasive

Remember the proverb from the story: "Words kill, words give life; they're either poison or fruit—you choose" (Proverbs 18:21 MSG).

It's easy to feel the natural urge to raise our voices when we want to get our point across, to speak hurtfully when we feel hurt, and to harm the ones closest to us because we assume they will forgive us. However, this is detrimental to so many relationships. Intensity kills intimacy.

What's hard to control is our reactions—especially at home, where we often feel most free to let our emotions run wild. However, taking the time to breathe, think, and gain composure before we react will always lead to fewer regrets and stronger, more loving relationships in the long run. Easier said than done, of course.

We've all been there, and almost all of us have room for improvement. For the exercise below, we'll work on just that.

Exercise

Think of the last time you lost your temper (or a good example that comes to mind). Put yourself back in that scene and answer the following questions as truthfully as you can.

What did you say?
_____
_____
_____
_____

How would you describe your tone?
_____
_____
_____
_____

What did you do (yell, roll your eyes, storm out, leave, etc.)?
_____
_____
_____
_____
_____
_____
_____
_____

Now, think of the situation from the other person's perspective. What could you have done differently, after viewing the situation from their side?

_____

_____

_____

_____

_____

_____

_____

_____

Think about how irrational you sounded in retrospect and when viewing the situation from the other person's perspective. What if you could do the same exercise during your next heated moment? Hint: you can!

Taking time to step away, breathe, and think through all sides of any disparity can afford you clarity to respond appropriately, like you might if you had the opportunity to look back on the situation, which you did in this exercise. And, scientifically speaking, removing yourself from a heated situation can allow the chemicals in your brain that cause stress and anger to dissipate, leading to a more calm and rational discussion to follow.

Next Steps

It's hard to anticipate the next time your opportunity to be persuasive versus abrasive will arise. Like John, it could come as quickly as a fallen fishbowl. However, here are three things you can do—before, during, and after the moment of impact—to help prepare you for the next time such an occurrence does inevitably happen:

- **Before—Develop an Exercise Routine:** If you don't already have one, consider incorporating an exercise routine into your daily schedule. In addition to boosting your overall health and well-being, cardio activity has also been proven to boost your brain's feel-good neurotransmitters, known as endorphins. You're less likely to "snap" with a less stressed, happier headspace, so go for a walk! Take up hiking. Try a dance class. Engage in whatever activity makes you feel good: mentally, physically, and beyond.
- **During—Give Others the Home Field Advantage:** As Willie mentioned (and as we discussed above), give your loved ones the benefit of the doubt. What if John, rather than getting upset at the lack of coffee in the house in the morning, considered the other ten tasks on Kristen's plate that may have led to her being unable to pick up coffee beans the day prior? The next time you're in a comparable situation,

take on the role of the "away team." In fact, make your home a place where you're always helping others win. It will change not only your conversations but your life.

- **After—Use "I" Statements:** When you apologize for anything, focus on framing everything as an "I" statement. "I'm sorry *I* got upset" rather than "I'm sorry *you* made me angry." Apologies should be about "I," not about putting the other person even further on the defensive.

Love First

Conclusion: How Will I Know When I'm Loving First?

Good work on completing the **Love First** Exercises! I hope you have also decided to apply many of the suggestions in the Next Steps sections into your daily life.

Now, how will you know that it's working? How will you know when you're truly loving first?

> ***When the people who know you the best love you the most.***

Sadly, many times the people who know us the best respect us the least because they truly see our flaws. It doesn't have to be this way. If you will truly seek to love first by demonstrating care, choosing to validate others, and approaching your spouse and children with gentleness, don't be surprised if the people who know you the best not only love you the most; they also begin to like you like never before.

Now, on to part 2 . . .

FUNDAMENTALS STEP 2

Live Last

As Willie told John, "Most people don't want to live last." The reality is, we are all self-centered by nature and it requires a decision to yield our rights for the good of another. However, when leaders think of others first in the workplace, it makes them someone others want to follow. The same is true at home. When a person chooses to help others win, it makes them a real winner!

What do you think it means to live last?

_____
_____
_____
_____
_____
_____
_____
_____
_____
_____
_____
_____

What do you think might be some hindrances to you living last?

_____
_____
_____
_____
_____
_____
_____
_____
_____
_____

Living last might not come naturally. As humans, we are predisposed to look out for ourselves first and others second. However, living last is the behavior that bolsters the belief that "My loved ones come first." If both partners in a relationship are living last, everybody wins.

Live Last

Things to Remember #1: Real Winners Show Up and Give Up So Others Can Go Up

In baseball, a player who bunts so a teammate can advance on the bases may not be the one who gets credit for scoring the run; however, he or she *is* the one who is responsible for the win. In the end, the most valuable player is the one who is willing to sacrifice the most.

Exercise

You likely didn't arrive where you are without the sacrifices of others. For this exercise, we're going to focus on those people. This can go as far back as you want—to childhood or earlier, before you ever knew what "sacrifice" meant.

In the first column below, list out those who have sacrificed for you: parents, relatives, teachers, coaches, friends, mentors, or your current family members. In the next column, list their sacrifice(s). Finally, think of how their actions affected your relationship and what you learned from them.

(If you need more rows, form another table on your own piece of paper—no sacrifice is too small to warrant mention!)

Name	Sacrifice(s)

Next Steps

There is an old saying that "those who drink the water should never forget those who dug the well." As you review the list of those who have sacrificed for you, remember we often are able to drink because someone else did the digging. Consider reaching out with a handwritten thank-you note, a call, or even a visit. If they are no longer living, make a commitment to pay it forward by modeling a sacrificial life toward those you love.

Effect on Relationship	What Did You Learn?

It's hard to plan out what you will sacrifice. Oftentimes, sacrifices are moment-by-moment decisions we may not even realize we're making. It's about taking small steps to cultivate an "others first" mentality. Here are a few of those possible steps:

- **Volunteer:** Again, sacrifice is hard. It may not be your first instinct. To train your brain in an "others first" mindset, begin regularly volunteering—even better if your family can join! Decide on a charity (or two) you are passionate about and find out how you can devote time (not just money!) to giving back monthly.

- **Find a Role Model:** Who is the most altruistic person you know? Take some time and think of a few names. If these are people you interact with in your daily life, make it a point to take them out to lunch. Ask them about their mindset when it comes to serving others, and take notes! If there are people on your list who aren't personally connected to you (e.g., famous martyrs), research them. Read their work. Learn from them and—again—take notes!
- **Focus on Active Listening:** Making sacrifices is especially hard if you don't know what sacrifices need to be made. Focus on active listening—on hearing what is said and what isn't. What do you pick up on in terms of where you could sacrifice more for your family?

Live Last

Things to Remember #2: See Need, Meet Need

Too often, we complicate life. We make little things into bigger ordeals than they need to be. We read too far into others' thoughts and intentions, creating unwarranted and unnecessary anxiety. And we overcomplicate how easy it can be to serve others.

When this happens, we must remember the basics: **see need, meet need**.

As Willie said, "What if you forgot about a list of marital obligations and just started looking for a need to meet. Anytime one showed up, no matter how large or small, you leveraged your time, energy, and effort to meet the need. What effect do you think it would have?"

There are two simple questions to ask yourself as you seek to **"see need, meet need"**:

1. Are you opening your eyes to see the needs present around you?
2. Are you taking the initiative to meet the needs once you see them?

If you're struggling with the first step, the exercise below should help!

Exercise

People rarely vocalize exactly what they need. Instead, needs may appear in the form of an overworked and exasperated spouse with a pile of dirty dishes in the sink, a lonely parent who is overly grateful for a phone call, or a grieving neighbor who you see receiving food deliveries. That's why you must be consciously looking for needs to be met: to take care of the dishes, call your parent more often, and occasionally cook a healthy meal for a neighbor in need.

Name	Need

THE FUNDAMENTALS

In the grid below, list the names of the people closest to you. Think about each one. What need do you think could be present that they're not saying? What can you do to fulfill that need? And, last, when will you do it by? Start by listening to what they are saying. Is there a place where they are demonstrating negative emotions? Do they appear tired? What brings them joy? Anytime we live with someone, we have the opportunity to pay attention to, and help meet, their needs.

Action	By When?

Next Steps

Copy the above grid onto a sheet of your own paper: Every. Single. Week.

Each week, identify at least three needs you can meet for others and expect nothing in return. (Because whether you receive recognition, reciprocation, or neither, you'll still experience joy in serving!)

Live Last

Things to Remember #3: Love Goes Slow

Love is like a three-legged race. Imagine what that looks like if one person is running and one is walking. A mess! Or, most likely, a pile of limbs on the ground.

In the words of Willie yet again, "Most leaders . . . feel a sense of urgency to chase their vision and conquer the mountain. If they're not careful, it's easy to run off and leave their people. But remember, *winning begins at home*. . . . The truth is, you can't be running if everyone else is walking, or you will leave them in the dust. Speed kills intimacy, my friend."

Exercise

Go back to your blueprint you created when we first discussed the Prerequisites on page 133. Rewrite your **Define What** and **Decide Why** here:

Define What:

_____

_____

_____

_____

Decide Why:

_____

_____

_____

_____

Now, schedule monthly check-in dates in your calendar when you will assess progress as you move toward your vision. Add the following questions to your calendar reminder:

1. Am I improving in moving toward the vision at every check-in?
2. Is our family moving together toward our vision?

Sometimes, we engage in actions we think are beneficial but are actually self-serving. If you can confidently answer yes to both questions above, congratulations. If not, make a list of ideas for how you can improve in the coming month.

Remember, progress over perfection. This isn't a race; it's a journey.

Next Steps

As you read in the introduction, everything you will work through in this book and Activation Guide will take time. No life-altering changes or groundbreaking improvements will happen overnight. Just as **love goes slow**, so, too, does development. Families that last aren't built fast. For the next steps to help love go slow, we will focus on helping you slow down *everything*. Test out these tactics and see how they improve your life:

- **Slow Down What Is Rushed:** What area of your life is often "rushed"? For many people, their answer is mornings. If this is the case for you, try waking up ten minutes earlier. Your body won't notice ten minutes' difference in sleep, but you will notice ten extra minutes for your morning routine! Worst case, you have too much time, in which case you can fill it with time to read, plan your day, or . . .
- **Read Scripture or Meditate to Begin Your Day.** Time devoted to reading something positive, prayer, or meditation has been proven to reduce stress, treat depression, and improve cognition.[6] Taking the time to practice either (or both!) can force you to slow down—and you'll reap extra benefits.
- **Try a Breathing Exercise:** According to the American Institute of Stress, abdominal breathing each day reduces stress and anxiety, supplies extra oxygen to the brain, and "stimulates the parasympathetic nervous system, which promotes a state of calmness."[7] Likewise, time

devoted to silence and solitude can set you up with a positive mindset to help you maintain perspective in your life at work and home.

- **Take a Vacation:** Reset with some time away to relax, refocus, and go slow. Your body, mind, and loved ones will surely thank you for it.

Live Last

Conclusion: How Will I Know When I'm Living Last?

Good work on completing the **Live Last** exercises! As with the Love First section, the benefits you will reap will not come from this book alone but in taking the practices into your daily life—starting with some of the suggested next steps for each "Things to Remember."

As you assess your progress, we must ask again: How will you know that it's working? How will you know when you're truly living last?

When everyone in your family is in front of you.

In a family, the goal is not to get to the destination fast; the goal is to get there together. The reality is, families that last aren't built fast. But they are built, and the starting point is when someone decides to lead from the back of the line. Why not choose to help someone else score by meeting needs and going at their pace? You might be surprised at how much better life is . . . together!

Now, for one final challenge . . .

Final Challenge

You should now know what it means—and what you have to do—to **love first** and **live last**. You have the blueprint in place to achieve the family you envision, and you have **defined what** you want and **decided why** you want it.

There is one final, important lesson Willie taught John: if something is controllable, winners dominate it.

You cannot control others' reactions, moods, or actions. You cannot control the uncontrollables of the world: the weather, the economy, or anything else left to chance.

But you can increase the likelihood of winning by dominating the controllables. The previous exercises and next steps should've shown you what is in your control.

For the final challenge, consider this: If you act on everything in your control, what does that look like? Write a letter to your future self, describing life when you dominate the controllables. The more detail, the better. Reference this letter every time you're struggling on your journey. Hopefully, the scene you describe will inspire you that although it may seem hard, it will always be worth it.

FINAL CHALLENGE

WINNING BEGINS AT HOME

Extra Credit

Let your loved ones read your letter. Invite them to join you on your journey and give them permission to hold you accountable to your vision. Let them see your commitment to understanding that *winning begins at home!*

ACKNOWLEDGMENTS

Whenever I read a book—and I read a bunch of them—I always read the acknowledgments because the truth is, there are no printed works without a team of people. To the following, my gratitude is immense:

First, to our team at Lead Every Day. I'm grateful to work with coaches who understand and help others Win Beyond Work. Scott B., Derek, Fred, Chal, Laci, Jeff, Ellen, and Karen: you all model living last. You are a dream team. And Becky, thank you for keeping us organized. You have been a Hulking Avenger to me for over two decades. To Scott Morgan, thank you for being a brother. Speaking of Avengers, you are Captain Love First. Heroes are in short supply, but you prove daily they still exist. The world is better for so many because you show up.

To Mark Miller, you challenged me to consider parables fifteen years ago. Thank you for all you have taught me about leadership and serving others. My life improved when we became friends! Dan Webster, I feel

ACKNOWLEDGMENTS

like the training wheels are off. Thanks to you, I found my way. I love you, my friend!

Thank you to Mark Levy (Levy Innovation), who helped me with the point of my ship. The idea for this book grew out of our weekend together over a decade ago. Jillian Broaddus (Buzz 84), I'm grateful. You worked diligently to make the Activation Guide better. You are so talented! To Janice Rutledge, I keep improving because of you. Thank you for hard feedback and easy friendship. Trey, and the team at Herald, thanks for partnering and connecting me to Batt. Every leader needs a Herald, and you are perfect for us. Elizabeth and Mckenzie (Storytold), thank you for helping us tell our stories. You both are pros. To the team at Maxwell Leadership and Forefront Books, wow! What an honor to work with your publishing team. To like-minded Justin Batt, who encouraged me from the start to be a voice to families, and Jen Gingerich and Christina Boys, who served as my editors. Jen, thanks for your patience, and Christina, neon tetras—really? You are a rock star! Jill Smith (you are incredible) and Lauren Ward, the author experience was amazing thanks to you and your team.

For me, *Winning Begins at Home* is rooted in a dream I have for everyone to have a great family. I know how much stability it brings because I had the privilege of growing up in one. My parents and grandparents were all married for more than fifty years. While they were far from perfect, we ate together, played together, and

ACKNOWLEDGMENTS

stayed together. I benefited greatly from Sunday visits and family suppers. Mom, you are still precious and still my hero. Your love and commitment to our family is priceless. Well done, Honey! Dad, I wish you were still here. I miss you every day, especially during baseball season. Thank you for being my coach and a fantastic dad. These great grandbabies would adore you!

Dorothy nailed it: "There's no place like home." Being a girl dad to four daughters *was the most fun I ever had*. Hannah, I love your focus. Sarah, I love your friendship. Rebekah, I love your fire. And Katherine, I love your fun. I have learned so much from being your dad. Thanks for overcoming my flaws. You are incredible daughters, wives, and now moms—women of virtue who hold my deepest affection. There's truly no greater joy than to know your children are walking in the Truth. To my four sons-in-law: may you live up to my expectations. They are high, but I'm confident Trevor, Bryan, Alex, and Airrion all have what it takes. I couldn't have handpicked better men to lead the next generation of our family. Stay pure, stay faithful, and stay! To my grandchildren and future generations: may you become men and women who love first and live last. Watch your parents; they will show you the way. Randad is your biggest fan!

Finally, to my wife, Laura. You are the one who makes me want to come home. Marrying you changed my life. I'm so grateful God chose you to be my partner.

ACKNOWLEDGMENTS

After nearly four decades, I love you more than ever. You are beautiful, creative, faithful, and the best wife, mom, and Lolly, without exception. Our family is a reflection of your faith. I love you!

Thank You, God, for coming up with the idea of marriage and family. When we follow Your plan, home is amazing. My prayer is that You will use *Winning Begins at Home* to make families better.

STAY CONNECTED

X: @randygravitt
IG: @randygravitt
LinkedIn: https://www.linkedin.com/in/randygravitt/

Podcast

The Lead Every Day Show

Company

For corporate training, coaching, and consulting, visit LeadEveryDay.com.

For speaking inquiries, visit RandyGravitt.com.

Email: randy@randygravitt.com

ABOUT THE AUTHOR

Randy Gravitt is an author, speaker, and executive coach who encourages leaders to reach their potential. Randy began his career working in education, both as a teacher and coach, before moving to Georgia, where he served for nearly two decades at one of the largest churches in the Atlanta area.

In 2014, Randy founded InteGREAT Leadership, which eventually became Lead Every Day. He currently serves as Lead Every Day's CEO (chief encouragement officer), leading a team of coaches and consultants who work with high-performance leaders, organizations, and teams around the world.

As a speaker, Randy delivers keynotes and training workshops on the topics of leadership, team building, organizational effectiveness, and peak performance. The organizations he has helped include Chick-fil-A, Grand Hyatt, Kroger, Fellowship of Christian Athletes, and the WinShape Foundation. Additionally, Randy has served

ABOUT THE AUTHOR

as one of the leadership speaker for the Pittsburgh Pirates and the Buffalo Bills organizations.

Randy has coauthored two books with Dan Webster, *Finding Your Way* and *Unstuck*. Both titles are aimed at helping leaders discover their passion and live fully engaged lives. Randy also encourages and equips leaders to win at work and home through the *Lead Every Day Show* with best-selling author Mark Miller.

Randy and his wife, Laura, have been married thirty-seven years and live in Sharpsburg, Georgia, where they raised their four daughters. Outside of work, Randy loves being a girl dad, hanging out with his grandkids, playing golf, reading, and sitting on his back porch.

Connect with Randy on social media @randygravitt or online at randygravitt.com.

ALSO BY RANDY GRAVITT

Finding Your Way: Discovering the Truth about You

by Randy Gravitt & Dan Webster

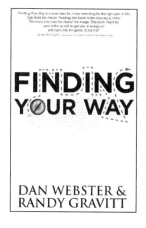

Have your ever wondered what you were born to do with your life? If you are at a point where you long to experience both fulfillment in your career and meaningful contribution in your circle of influence, *Finding Your Way* will position you to live an integrated life that leads to maximum impact.

ALSO BY RANDY GRAVITT

Unstuck: A Story about Gaining Perspective, Creating Traction, and Pursuing Your Passion

by Randy Gravitt & Dan Webster

Untwist the question mark from your life to start living authentically. *Unstuck* offers a path forward for those who are "stuck"—despite the comfort, security, and what *should* feel like success. Do you feel disengaged from a life that looks good on paper? Do you sense there *must* be something more?

- ◆ Rethink your purpose in life and discover your calling
- ◆ Rediscover the truth about yourself and who you really want to be
- ◆ Follow a clear formula for moving forward with authenticity
- ◆ Break out of your comfort zone and feel fully alive

Through the story of George Johnson, a man in a position much like yourself, you'll learn how to shed the boredom, emptiness, and confusion so you can get on with your life. Whether you need a complete overhaul or just a jump start, *Unstuck* will help you make it happen!

NOTES

1. "Disengagement Persists among U.S. Employees," Gallup, accessed February 28, 2024, https://www.gallup.com/workplace/391922/employee-engagement-slump-continues.aspx.
2. Maddy Savage, "Why Promoted Women Are More Likely to Divorce," BBC, January 22, 2020, https://www.bbc.com/worklife/article/20200121-why-promoted-women-are-more-likely-to-divorce.
3. "Stress in America™: Paying With Our Health." American Psychological Association, February 4, 2015. https://www.apa.org/news/press/releases/stress/2014/stress-report.pdf.
4. "Gartner HR Survey Reveals 88% of Organizations Have Encouraged or Required Employees to Work from Home Due to Coronavirus," Gartner, March 19, 2020, https://www.gartner.com/en/newsroom/press-releases/2020-03-19-gartner-hr-survey-reveals-88--of-organizations-have-e.
5. Lauren Dunn, "Be Thankful: Science Says Gratitude Is Good for Your Health," Today, November 26, 2015,

NOTES

   https://www.today.com/health/be-thankful-science-says-gratitude-good-your-health-t58256.
6. Jeena Cho, "6 Scientifically Proven Benefits of Mindfulness and Meditation," *Forbes*, July 14, 2016, https://www.forbes.com/sites/jeenacho/2016/07/14/10-scientifically-proven-benefits-of-mindfulness-and-meditation/.
7. Kellie Marksberry, "Take a Deep Breath," American Institute of Stress, August 10, 2012, https://www.stress.org/take-a-deep-breath.